ACADEMIC LIBRARIANSHIP
A PERSPECTIVE

ACADEMIC LIBRARIANSHIP
A Perspective

R. SREEPATHY NAIDU

Foreword by
Prof. KRISHAN KUMAR

GIAN PUBLISHING HOUSE
NEW DELHI - 110002

GIAN PUBLISHING HOUSE
4-C Ansari Road
New Delhi 110002

ISBN 81—212—0271—X

PRINTED IN INDIA

Published by Mrs. Gayatri Garg for Gian Publishing House, New Delhi and
Printed at : Goyal Offset Printers Delhi-35 Ph. 535881

Dedicated

to

MY BELOVED PARENTS

FOREWORD

In our times, there has been unparalleled growth of information, unprecedented developments in technology, and cuts in librarye budgets. As a result, libraries have become increasingly complex and difficult to manage. Librarians are faced with immens problems. This is especially true of university libraries. Today managing a large university library effectively requires management skills on the part of a university librarian. In addition, a university librarian has to be a highly knowledgeable person about the world of books. It can be said of Shri R. Sreepathy Naidu that he has been a successful librarian, devoted to his job. Looking back he can feel satisfaction in having given his best to the academic community in particular academic librarianship.

The author has vast experience of working in a university library and teaching library and information science. In October 1988 he has completed 32 years of service at Sri Venkateswara University. He has utilized his valuable experience to write papers on different aspects of librarianship covering college and university libraries ; library and information science education ; library buildings ; user education ; building library collection ; library legislation ; libraries in USA, UK, East Germany and France. His experience and insight into problems of university and college libraries can provide guidance to young librarians, who can benefit greatly from his wide knowledge, experience and expertise.

Shri Naidu is to be congratulated for attempting to bring together his contributions on different aspects of librarianship. The book will prove to be a valuable addition to Indian literature on Library and information science.

Professor of Library & Information Science, Delhi University, Delhi.

KRISHAN KUMAR

PREFACE

The author has proud privilege in bringing this volume to the hands of professional friends—men and women from all over the country whose individual efforts and aspirations have earned the respect and recognition to the profession that it occupies today. In a bid to select an appealing caption for the present volume, the one that has been chosen "Academic Librarianship : A Perspective" appears to be appropriate as the contents reflect the broad theme.

During the professional career of the author spanning over 35 years in different spheres of Librarianship as a teacher and as a Library manager, about two scores of articles published are abound with practical wisdom. The articles selected may not be directly useful to the serious students of Library Science nor does it claim to be a reference work. However, this will bring about a good experience to the professionals and working Librarians.

The articles are grouped into four categories viz. (a) Published articles, (b) Conference papers, (c) Chapters published in books authored by other professional colleagues and, (d) personal observations made during the visits to western countries. Also included in this section are some of the reports submitted to bodies like University Grants Commission for follow up action.

It is hoped and trusted that this volume would stimulate further thinking to help Librarianship gain new dimensions and reach new heights.

R. SREEPATHY NAIDU

PREFACE

THE author has proud privilege in bringing this volume to the hands of professional friends—men and women—from all over the country whose individual efforts and aspirations have earned the respect and recognition of the profession that it occupies today. In a bid to select an appealing caption for the present volume, the one that has been chosen "Academic Librarianship: A Perspective" appears to be appropriate as the contents reflect the broad theme.

During the professional career of the author spanning over 35 years in different spheres of Librarianship as a teacher and as Library manager, about two scores of articles published are abound with practical wisdom. The articles selected may not be directly useful to the graduate students of Library Science nor does it claim to be a reference work. However, this will bring about a good experience to the professionals and working Librarians.

The articles are grouped into four categories viz. (a) Published articles, (b) Conference papers, (c) Chapters published in books authored by other professional colleagues and (d) Personal observations made during the visits to foreign countries. Also included in this section are some of the reports submitted to bodies like University Grants Commission for follow up action.

It is hoped and trusted that this volume would stimulate further thinking to help Librarianship add new dimensions and reach new heights.

[illegible] NAIDU

ACKNOWLEDGEMENTS

Many good friends have helped me in various ways in the writing and production of this book and my gratitude is expressed to my professional colleagues in the Library as well as in the department of Library Science ; administrative staff for getting manuscript typed and Xeroxed. I am greatly indebted to Prof. Krishan Kumar who is gracious enough to scribe a Foreword. Lastly I am very much beholden to the publishers M/s Gian Publishing House who have taken up the printing, publication in record time.

CONTENTS

KNOWLEDGE
Expansion, Explosion and Exploration

In the beginning of the world there was no system of learning and teaching, nor was there any book to read. As such, it was not possible for anybody to acquire knowledge without receiving instruction from God who was the primary source of all the true knowledge and of all that was known. So, God gave His own knowledge for the benefit of all men. God revealed it to the consciousness of four *rishis*, (inspired seers), namely, *Agni*, *Vayu*, *Aditya* and *Angiras* in the shape of four *Vedas*—the *Rig Veda*, the *Yajurveda*, the *Sama Veda* and the *Atharva Veda*. The word 'Veda' is derived from the root 'Vida' to know, and, therefore, *Vedas* are the sources of knowledge. The great semetic religions also refer to God as the first Teacher, Man when they say that He taught Adam the names of things.

In the *Vedas* subjects as widely varied as Theology, Sociology, Ethics, Metaphysics, Architecture, Mathematics, Astronomy Aeronautics etc., are incorporated. According to Prof. Max-Mueller, the great German scholar, the *Vedas* will take and maintain for ever the position as the most ancient of books in the library of mankind. In the Vedic age the people worshipped at the shrine of the 'word' with reverence for it contained the germ of Divinity. The ancient sages and even modern Indian scholars maintain that the *Vedas* contain the seeds of all true knowledge. According to Yagnavalkya, there are fourteen *Vidyas* (branches of knowledge) which are included in the *Vedas*. Besides these, there are four additional subjects, namely *Ayurveda* or science of life including medicine, *Dhanurveda* or military science, *Gandharva Veda* or science of music and *Atharva Veda* or science and practice of mechanical arts, also called *Shilpa vidya*. The chief aim of the Vedas is to teach the mankind.

In India, recording of knowledge started much earlier than in any other countries. The history of India is the story of the ancient civilization of the world. Humanity like individual started classifying knowledge even in its very infancy. This is quite clear from the division of the *Vedas* into four portions, namely :

1. *Rig Veda—Jnana kanda* (Knowledge portion) (Dealing with the knowledge of things)
2. *Yajur Veda—Karma kanda* (Action portion) (Dealing with the knowledge of action)
3. *Sama Veda—Upasana kanda* (Devotion or worship portion) (Dealing with the spiritual knowledge)
4. *Atharva Veda—Vigyan kanda* (Science, spiritual and material) (Dealing with science and material)

The Vedic system divided the universe of subjects into four main subjects, viz., *Dharma*, *Artha*, *Kama* and *Moksha* corresponding to the four fundamental values of the same names. The sequence of the four groups corresponds to the different stages through which the society or an individual tends to move. The vedic system of the division of the universe of subjects or organization of knowledge is thus socio-centred.

This grouping or arrangement covers the following subjects :

(i) Dharma : (Righteous conduct)—Law, Theology, (Religion), Ethics and Sociology—the subjects involved in the maintenance of society as coherent organization.

(ii) Artha : (Wealth and Prosperity)—History, Political Science, Economics and the Applied Sciences—subjects leading to structural and social welfare.

(iii) Kama : (Noble aspirations)—Literature, Fine Arts and Pure Sciences—subjects arising out of the fulfilment of the creative urge in man and for the enjoyment of the results of such creation.

(iv) Moksha: (Emancipation)—Philosophy and Spiritual Experiences—subjects for understanding the universe by intellect and thereby getting over the miseries of life and attaining peace and emancipation or release from the bondage of birth and death.

In Dr. Johnson's words, "knowledge is of two kinds. We know a subject ourselves, or we know we can find information upon it." It is in relation to the latter part of the quotation that the fundamentals of Reference service or Reference work take shape. It is obviously a logical outgrowth of the phenomenal expansion of the field of knowledge, of the intellectual upheaval of modern times and of the democratic conviction of the freedom of access to such knowledge and information. Although reference work has long been acknowledged as basic to an efficient Library service, the current trends lay an increased emphasis on the side of the readers—the readers who have multiplied due to population explosion—the readers who have to face another unique phenomena of modern times that is, the publication explosion. Increase in the number of library users, spread of education, and the ever-increasing urge for learning and knowing have established Reference work on a high pedestal in the hierarchy of Library Science. Today's Librarian has to "approach the field of Library Science from the side of the readers"—(Ranganathan). This is the field where Reference Librarian works.

With the expansive modern concept and definition his horizon has definitely widened, transcending perhaps the limit of his resources, in terms of service potential and control of material, sweeping away the traditional concept. It is not merely his question-answering duties performed with the help of a few conventional tools in the traditional sense, today it is his all-out effort to satisfy his clientele's reading, research and informational needs. He has now to work with his entire library collection and even with extra library resources. Increased emphasis on special library work and the rise of technical information centres have added a new edge to reference service.

'All men by nature seek to know', so observed Aristotle over 2000 years ago. Throughout the ages, men have sought knowledge of the seas and planets, of growing things, of the ways things work, and of man himself. Men seek to know of the atom's secrets and the mysteries of medicine, of music and machines, and of the ways of life of men in distant lands. They seek further knowledge of the earth, the skies and the space beyond. As more and more men seem to learn the things that books can teach and as this hunger for knowledge swells and spreads, a long felt need grows all the greater ; the need for many books within the reach of all men. To serve this need, expanding with the ever-widening boundaries of knowledge itself, is the challenge and the dedicated purpose of the libraries.

It has rightly been stated that the road to freedom begins at the doors of knowledge. Freedom of knowledge lends strength to

all the freedoms. Without knowledge and understanding even the very meaning of freedom is often elusive. Today, perhaps as never before, men need the opportunities to read for themselves and to think for themselves to judge and to make decisions and to understand their fellowmen. It goes without saying that the status of a Nation as a whole depends upon the welfare and achievements of the people irrespective of social class, sex and religion. The welfare of the masses, in turn, depends on their education and way of thinking. The best way of improving the welfare of the people is to democratize knowledge through a network of free schools and supplemented by nation-wide free library service. Library service is a positive and aggressive dynamic force to spread knowledge in every nook and corner of the country and to make it available for the individual.

According to M.L. Wilson, Director of extension work of the U.S. Department of Agriculture, "In view of the current world situation, the reading of books and journals has never been so important as it is today. Through them we have the privilege of exploring and finding out ourselves. They offer a solid background of knowledge ; help us to meet the practical demands of our business ; set new views and ideas before us ; and they lay the thinking and knowledge of the entire world before us where we can select what meet our needs, instead of having it selected for us."

Carl R. Woodward, President of Rhode Island, said ; "Books are the instruments for perpetuating the body of knowledge painfully and slowly accumulated through the ages of man. They are also the means of preserving and sustaining the solid foundations of culture and learning. They provide the record of man's progress and the point of departure for steps into the future. Through them the cultural resources of mankind become the birth right of generations to come."

Books give us inspiration. Knowledge unused is like dead lumber, constantly in our way. We need the will to quicken the resources we have. This is inspiration.

Books are the legacies that a great genius leaves to mankind, which are delivered down from generation to generation, as presents to the posterity of those who are yet to unborn.

Ours is an age of 'explosions'. The explosion which reigns supreme is the 'knowledge explosion'. The driving forces which gave birth to this explosion are varied and many. Important among them are (i) the remarkable progress made by science and technology during the last 150 years or so ; (ii) the democratization of political institutions throughout the world ; (iii) the popularization of education in all sections of society; (iv) the introduction of speedy means of communications, such as, telephone, radio, television and supersonic jets etc., (v) the race for supremacy in space research among the advanced nations ; (vi) the competition in trade and industry among various nations ; (vii) the impact of Russian Revolution in 1917 which provided the impetus for research in social sciences ; (viii) the impact of Two World Wars in 1914-18 and 1939-45 ; (ix) the emergence of nationalism in the Asian and African countries ; (x) the improvement in printing technology and paper-making ; and (xi) the establishing of the United Natio and its specialized agencies, including UNESCO.

These forces naturally had a tremendous impact on the establishment of libraries, research institutions and documentation centres throughout the world. They are also responsible for the production of a large number of survey reports, books and journals. According to an estimate, about 5 lakh books and 80,000 periodicals were published in the year 1972 throughout the world. In India alone, 22,096 books were published in the financial year 1975-76. As a consequence of this unprecedented rise in book-production during the last 50 years or so, the world's largest libraries have millions of books and journals for the use of research workers and scientists.

As far as the number of libraries in India is concerned, there are more than 20,000 libraries of all description in the country, including eight libraries attached to institutions declared by the Parliament to be of national importance and over 1000 specialized libraries attached to various departments of the Central and State Governments. There are also specialized libraries providing facilities for researchers. The more prominent among them are at the Indian Council of World Affairs, New Delhi ; the Indian Statistical Institute Calcutta ; the Gokhale Institute, Pune ; the Theosophical Society, Madras ; the National Council of Applied Economic Research, New Delhi ; and the Indian Institute of Public Administration, Delhi. Some other leading libraries are the Delhi Public Library (5 lakh volumes) and the Central Secretariat Library (4 lakh volumes). Apart from these, some of the bigger universities also have sizeable collections.

Turning to the expansion of education in India and the establishment of University and College Libraries, the number of universities rose from 47 in 1960 to 101 in 1973 and again to 119 in 1978-79 with an enrolment of 3.86 million during the same period. The number of colleges increased from 1542 in 1960-61 to 3604 in 1970-71 and rose again to 4460 in 1979-80 and 4886 in 1981-82. These statistics abundantly prove that India too has a major share in the 'knowledge explosion', and in order to cope with this, each university and college has equipped its library with the desired materials. The 'knowledge explosion' has great influence on the research activities in our country. For instance, in 1952-53 the country spent Rs. 122 million on research and development. By 1971-72 the figure had gone upto Rs. 2150 million and by 1979-80 the expenditure was shot up to 600 crores (6000 million). For 1980-81 the revised estimate was Rs. 7261 million. (Centre Sector Rs. 5722, State and Private Sector Rs. 1037 (million).

THE LIBRARY

For Enrichment of Teaching

A Library is now recognised as an important social institution in the life of any community where every person can seek every kind of knowledge. With the development in the art of production of recorded knowledge, libraries are extended in size and enlarged their services. An academic library, therefore, is an important educational tool in the realm of higher education. No Science college can function without laboratories. A laboratory in a college serves only a branch of knowledge whereas a Library contains material in all branches of knowledge.

It is appropriate to quote here what J. Loab has stated as far back in 1923 regarding the importance of library. "Real discoveries are actually made in the library and subsequently tested out in the laboratory."

The importance of library in the sphere of higher education has been stressed by every University Education Commission. In the report of Dr. Radhakrishnan, in 1948, he has emphasised that "Training in higher branches of learning and research is merely a question of learning how to use the tools and if the library tools are not there ; how can the student learn to use them ? President Truman's Commission on Higher Education says—"The Library is second only to the instructional staff in its importance for high quality of instruction and research". Therefore, a present college should have well planned, functional library so that the graduate, leaving Institutions, may be able to meet the increasing demands of the individual intelligence and intellectual capabilities in the changing social political and economic conditions in our country.

We are fully aware of the causes for the unhappy situation existing in the administration and organisation of a purposeful Library, to suit the demands of higher education. To mention a few the following may be the reasons :

(a) The management and administrator have not realised that Library is an integral part of a college since there is confusion of purpose ;
(b) Meagre financial resources ;
(c) Ignoring the appointment of qualified and competent Librarian ;
(d) Inadequate Library accommodation ;
(e) Curriculum and methods of instructions ;
(f) Uninterested faculty members ;
(g) Lack of love of reading in the student community.

So I need not once again over-emphasize in detail the above reasons as we are quite conscious of the lacunae. Few Institutions realise the importance of a congenial and cohesive Library.

Teaching is a noble profession as such the teacher should be nobler and be emulated by others. So, the entire community revolve round the teacher and his teaching. Teaching is an art ; needs a thorough preparation and real dedication to the profession. The method of teaching and mode of explanation, convincing the students depend on using the Library profusely. In my opinion the real teaching to capture the student's attention should be to absorb the students into confidence and convince them with proper approach. So, the methodology should be to brief the topic at the first instance; to give an exhaustive lecture ; comprehend the facts and figures relevant to the topic ; to make the students question the teacher on the topic so far dealt, which would reveal the depth of understanding by the students, and lastly to assign a few references for the follow-up work. If this is sincerely followed, I am quite sure that not only the relation between the teacher and the taught grows up but also the impression on the students would be indelible. Of course the teaching methodology may differ from teacher to teacher and from institution to institution. However, I am quite confident that the above type of methodology can be kept up if the teacher conserves the knowledge by using the Library with true perspective as well as making the students utilise the resources of the Library in their own way with the references assigned.

My assumptions of education are as follows :

1. That we ought to produce self-reliant individuals capable of choice and of individual thought rather than human sheep.
2. That education can be a means of fostering the development of such individuals.
3. That what people read can be an important means of education both in the formal sense and informal use of leisure-sense.
4. That there are difference in quality of reading matter.

Thus, the books suggested by the teachers should not be of any mean quality but should be most comprehensive in coverage and qualitative facts contained. Therefore, a good book should be of convincing in its kind rather naturalistic or fantastic, stimulating to the imagination, rich in ideas, sound in values with structure and expression entirely in harmony with content and capable of 'stretching' the young reader, i.e. providing a satisfying experience. In the words of Dr. S.R. Ranganathan, National Professor of Library Science ; "Education is the process of the development of a personality along its own lines and its own speed, to its own fullness, the chief agencies playing part in the education of an individual (student), the individual specifically helping the process of education (teacher) and the total environment (Physical, biological and social)". Thus, the education of good individual can be helped by any element in a totality of his environment. In modern times, Library and books form one of the essential elements in that environment. The purpose of education must be to inspire reading interest in persons and to sharpen their intellect but the lack of reading interest witnessed in the present day children has contributed to the present system of text-book centered education, have influenced the attitudes of teachers, parents etc. in discouraging the reading habit of the students outside the prescribed text-books. The methods of instruction adopted by the teachers are examination-oriented, emphasising on the mark securing devices, thus, compelling the students to take to cheap bazaar notes and guides. The management and the administrator, above all, the public often reminds the academic students of the college on the percentage of the results. This defeats the very purpose of the higher education and kills the intiative and the interests of the students. No one has bothered above this. So a student finds no need to visit the Library, except probably to scan the dailies or to disturb a friend of his studying in the quiet corners of the reading room. Thus, the main stream of the visitors to the Library, the students, is almost cut off from the Library. There is not that real diffusion of knowledge to compel the students to discover the source of the information in the Library.

Thus, among the faculty members, a few uninterested are observed who often consider themselves as mere wage earners who are not utilising the services of education tools in the Library to improve their own intellectual capacities or class room work. They function merely as transmitters of information to the students and are content in completing the set syllabus, feeling quite satisfied and probably as a sign of relief. No attempt is made by them to create a real, genuine love of reading in the student. As a result, the student does not carry with him the capacity of the taste for serious study and living interest in the books and so finds no need even to visit the Library.

In conclusion let me point out that the Library is indeed an external memory i.e, the books and the documents socialised for this purpose. The teacher should create curiosity in his students to find out facts and ideas from the reserves of the Library. The teachers' function in the class-room is to stimulate curiosity in the students sufficiently and direct them to the Library for further sharpening of the intellect. Sharpening of the intellect can be done through class-room discussions, tutorial meetings. It is a duty of the Librarian to organise the reading materials in such a way that our student gets what he needs pinpointedly, exhaustively and expeditiously. Thus, the teachers and Librarians should work as partners for the intellectual growth of the students. Now, there arises the necessity of organising orientation lectures in initiating the fresh students at the beginning of every academic year, to throw open the Library into 'open access' giving full choice to browse the resources of the Library ; to arrange for study circles and group discussion on and often on relevent topics, and to develop techniques of seminars and building up of home Libraries.

I am also of the opinion that the syllabus at various levels of education should be so oriented as to bring out a cordial relationship between the teaching and the Library use. Even the examination system should also be so designed to permit the students to write the exams., with open books which would certainly help the students to use un-sparingly the references given for assignments in the class-room. Answering the questions with open books, referring to relevant topics from among the sources, books should also be awarded marks.

Lastly let me suggest the following few points which would help to improve the quality of the higher education :

(a) Replacement of mass lectures by individual instruction;
(b) Replacement of memory-filling by development of thinking power ;
(c) Replacement of text-book-centered, teacher-centered education by Library-centered, child-centered education ;
(d) Replacement of the present mode of examination of question answers by question box as suggested by U.G.C. and "Open book" system ;
(e) Replacement of secretive and competitive outlook by the spirit of team-work and relay work among the students.

This should be so extended to the College and University level that teachers and Librarians should be partners in order to maximise the productivity of the education. In this context let me quote the words of Mahatma Gandhi : "Real Education consists in training the best of yourself, what better work can there be than the book of humanity", Similarly Colton has stated about the value of books "Next to acquiring good friends the best acquisition is that of good books".

STUDY HABITS

Effective Use of Library

Reading can be achieved through education. In the words of Dyer "Reading means : *Any grasp of a written page with a modicum of understanding.*" That is why Education is defined as the ability to read and to create reading. It implies that an educated person must not only possess the good reading habit but also the capacity to stimulate reading in others. Constant and serious reading in a way develops the mental growth of the readers. As our Late Prime Minister Nehru puts it "*The reading habit should be developed with the thinking habit. If people give up reading habit obviously they become lopsided and cease to grow.*" Study strictly means serious and critical reading which demands concentration of the person.

Reading then means casual study of reading materials like newspapers, fiction etc. The reading habit is considered the voluntary activity. In reality, the creation of this habit depends upon various factors, viz., 1) Attitude of teachers in the class room ; 2) Temperament of the parents ; 3) Attitude of children ; 4) Availability of reading materials. In ancient times, when the written language and alphabet were unknown, knowledge was communicated from one generation to another and one person to another orally through *Gurukula* system of Education. In the absence of art of writing, there was no scope for the development of Education as is being witnessed today. The introduction of alphabet for expressing thoughts in writing made it possible to keep the knowledge in the form of documents which were in palm-leaf. Since the wealthy could afford to possess these documents, education was restricted to a privileged few. The modern period which saw the manufacture of paper and invention of printing, brought up books that have been multiplied in greater number speedily and at cheaper cost.

Thus, the rapid production of books paved the way for the advancement of Education. Further, the democratic forms of governments which came to power realised the need to make the people literate and educated for achieving economic prosperity and national development. As such, education was made compulsory for all the people up to a certain level. Keeping in view the significance of education and its impact over the advancement of the country, our Government has encouraged the development of education at all levels by providing the necessary financial assistance. With this, more and more people became literates. Further the ample opportunities and facilities available to one and all for pursuing higher education (University education) without any discrimination whatsoever, led to advancement of learning and specialisation in various branches of knowledge. The specialisation or research activity in any field of study can be possible only through constant study of the latest development and findings in their subject field reported in the latest publication i.e. Books and periodicals. Research necessitates thinking capacity and intellectual development which can be possible only through cultivation of the regular reading habit. Since the reading habit is the outcome of education, it may not be out of place here to know what education means and its impact on society.

As Dr. D.J. Reddy has aptly put it in his book *Challenges in Higher Education* "Education is like a social birth ; it gives man a social and cultural existence. Education is the privilege of man. Animals may be trained but never educated. Education is a way by which societies keep alive and pass on their knowledge, and institutions to the next generation. Education in short preserves Society."

In the words of late Dr. S.R. Ranganathan, National Professor of Library Science, Govt. of India : "Education is the Process of the development of a personality along its own lines and its own speed, to its own fullness ; the Chief agencies playing part in the education of an individual (Educand), the individual specifically helping the process of education (Teacher) and the total environment (Physical, Biological and Social)". Thus, the education of an individual can be helped by any element in the totality of his environment. In modern times, libraries and books form one of the essential elements in that environment. The purpose of education must be to inspire reading interests in persons and to sharpen their intellect. But the lack of reading interest witnessed in the present day children is attributed to the present system of text book centred education which influenced the attitudes of the teachers, parents etc. in discouraging the reading habit of the students outside the prescribed text books.

Attitude of Parents : The creation of reading habit in children will also to a certain extent depend upon the attitude of their parents towards education. At one extreme, the few parents who use libraries extensively themselves encourage their children to do likewise, support the growth of libraries and regard them as a major educational force. At another extreme, there are many parents who take little interest in reading and do not make their children feel about the importance of the Libraries. Theoretically the majority of the parents agree to the value of reading. But in reality, they hold the view that the present system of education is only for passing of examinations in order to obtain a certificate as a passport to a job. In view of this, most of the parents insist on their children, studying prescribed text books, for preparing for examinations instead of spending their time in libraries for furthering their knowledge. Unless the necessary changes are effected to modify the present system of teaching and examination, the attitude of parents will remain the same.

Attitude of Teachers : Many teachers express a strong belief in the educational importance of the libraries, and attach a high value to them in theory but had little to do with them in educational practice. The present method of education is characterised as teacher-transmitted education. In this system, the teacher is vested with the responsibility of teaching his pupils according to the prescribed syllabus and text books. Since the worthiness of the teacher is judged by the percentage of success in the examination based on set text books, the teacher is compelled to instruct his students exclusively to fulfil the academic achievements in conformity with the recommended syllabus.

The pressure of examinations, the demands of the curriculum, limited time available for teaching makes it difficult for the teachers to educate children in the use of the libraries. The predominance of the mode of examination has restricted the reading habit of students to a few recommended text books covering the course.

This does not help true education. It kills curiosity and retards mental growth. One of the essential aids to such a mental growth is wide and continuous reading of books. The present system of examination is designed essentially to test memory, which reacts on the teaching methods. Even in the case of problems that require discussion and arguments, the very arguments were dictated as notes. To increase productivity not only the teaching methods but also the examination system need be reformed in such a way as to transform the teaching method from that of memory-filling to that or intellect-sharpening. The correct method of teaching should be to minimise the lecture hours and allow the students to equip themselves by individual as well as team work in the Library. This reform is necessary to increase the productivity of our education. Education must be productive, and Dr. D.J. Reddy expressed it as follows : "Education is not accumulating of facts as Libraries and other media of communication could do it better and so, not a package of information. Education is preparation for productive work and to make living graceful."

Attitude of Children : Reading is considered a voluntary activity. The urge for reading emanates through that type of teaching which can stimulate thinking. Knowledge is not hereditary and intuitive. If so, there will not be any necessity to acquire knowledge by reading books in the Library. The reading habit can best be formed during childhood and adolescence and seldom later. At home the parents must necessarily initiate their children in the use of books and create such congenial atmosphere suitable to kindle reading interest in them and promote their continuous reading. The teacher is regarded as a walking encyclopaedia. Children feel that they need not learn anything beyond the class room teaching. The more thoroughly and efficiently they are taught, the less need there seems to be for reading other than the prescribed text books. Further Sports and Games, Audio-visual materials which attract their attention make them less interested in reading. Unless changes are made in the system of education as to test the intellectual capacity of the students, the children will have little interest in reading.

In view of the above facts, it will be clear that the present system of text-book oriented education and memory-testing method of examination prevents either the teacher in the class room or the parents at home to make the children library-minded. Hence the aim of education must be to inculcate reading habit. The good and wide reading of reading materials widen the horizons of one's knowledge and develop his thinking power. In order to keep the reading habit alive, books must be made accessible. Books are the vehicles of thought in which are recorded the knowledge of the thinkers of the past and present. In the opinion of Dr. D.J. Reddy "Books and friends are a treasure; their value and influence are realised only when they are lost." The use of books will influence the thinking and shape the mental outlook of the users. The reading of books will affect one's thought and behaviour. If education makes the persons literate, books will make them enlightened and cultured. Thus the Libraries supplement education. In order to meet the requirements of those inclining to read, there must be some institution to collect, store, arrange the books in a systematic order to make them easily accessible and to interpret the resources available to the users through the personal service of the staff members. That institution will be known as the Library.

In ancient times the Library was concerned as a store house of books when the learning was limited and the books were meant only for preservation and not for use. The use of paper, the introduction of printing facilitated the rapid production of books which changed the conception of the Library. In modern conception, Library came to be regarded as a treasure house or the temple of knowledge and as an institution of social education where books are acquired and arranged for use of all. Since it is vital for the intellectual and cultural development of the people, the Library of to-day is referred to as the *University of the People* freely accessible to one and all.

It has been often pointed out that the word LIBRARY has two usages. One to describe a collection of books and the other to describe the normal location of such a collection, and in that the two do not necessarily always run together.

The Library is a combination of three factors, the readers, the reading materials (Books) and the library staff. The service which establishes the intimate relation among the three factors of the Library is technically known as *Library Service*. Library is a place to pursue knowledge, perhaps following some special interest or quite consciously as a means of self-improvement. Library as a source of independent learning is being neglected because education is so often a passive absorption of teacher-transmitted education.

Consequently the educational significance of the libraries in the promotion of reading good books outside the school hours among the children is ignored. In order to get the library effectively used, it is desirable to have school libraries with good and appropriate books manned by technically qualified persons. This can be effected by establishing due coordination between the teachers and Librarians.

The teacher should stimulate each and every pupil to go to the Library and to draw by himself every possible help from that intellectual deposit (viz. Library). The Librarian on his part will assume the educational responsibility in organising the reading materials properly and systematically. He will also introduce latest techniques in respect of reading sklls and study methods. Thus the combined efforts of teacher and Librarian will maximise the productivity of education.

The interpretation of books in the classroom should arouse sufficient curiosity in the student. They should be habituated to use the Library throughout their lives. The Librarian should play an equally important role in guiding the students in the selection of books and in providing necessary facilities for reading within the Library. Thus, the teacher and the Librarian should cooperate in organising and correlating the work in the class room and the Library.

The Library is indeed externalised memory i.e. the books and other documents socialised for this purpose. The teacher should create curiosity in his students to find out facts and ideas from the Library. That is, the teacher's function in the class room is to stimulate curiosity in the students sufficiently and direct them to the library for further sharpening of the intellect. Sharpening of intellect can be done through class room discussions, tutorial meetings etc. It is the duty of the Librarian to organise the reading materials in such a way that each student gets what he needs pinpointedly, exhaustively and expeditiously. Thus, the teachers and librarians should work as partners for the intellectual growth of the students.

Necessity of Orientation Lecture : Students need be initiated by the Librarian in the use of the library for making effective use of the same. Since various techniques are adopted in the library to mechanise the arrangements of books and retrieval of information the users need some guidance and knowledge of how to use the Library. This can be done by making the librarian conduct the orientation lecture to familiarise them with the library techinques.

The teachers should permit their students to attend the orientation lecture.

Open Access System : The Libraries are known as the intellectual deposits of the past. The clientele will not be in a position to make use of the Library unless they are given free access to the books. Browsing of books itself will make a person to cultivate the habit of reading. Books widen one's insight and thought and help one to think of other things than one's own interests. In the words of Mahatma Gandhi *Real Education consists in drawing the best of yourself; what better work can there be than the book of humanity.* Similarly Colton has stated as follows about the value of books : "Next to acquiring good friends, the best acquisition is that of good books." Thus the introduction of free access to books is one way of effecting the use of the Library.

Study Circles : The formation of study circles will help the students to discuss among themselves and to exchange their views over the chosen topics which will enrich their knowledge.

Reference service is indispensable in the promotion of reading habit and use of books where the contact is established between the right reader and the right book at a right time by the personal service of the library staff. The readers will not be in a position to know which of the books will be useful to their tastes. To interpret the resources of the Library and enlighten them about the location of required information, Reference service is carried out in the Library. Thus, the personal contact of the staff with the students will attract them to the Library.

Seminars and Home Libraries : Conducting of elocution competitions, essay competitions and Seminars will also encourage the students to make use of the Library. Further, necessary facilities have to be created for encouraging the maintenance of home Library by the parents to encourage reading habit to children.

Assignment of good number of exercises on different topics and examinations with open books will also compel the students to be in constant touch with the books, thus making them Library-conscious.

The Librarian on his part must master his techniques and act like a doctor of books, a mixture of scholar and Public Relations Officer who makes active use of his specialised knowledge to bring people closer together, an expert consultant for people on books and an interpreter of books to people.

The advancement of education and the effective use of the

Library to put it briefly depends upon the adherence of the following suggestions made by Dr. S.R. Ranganathan, National Professor of Library Seience.

1. Replacement of mass-lecture by individual instruction ;
2. Replacement of memory-filling by Development of thinking power ;
3. Replacement of text-book-centred, teacher-centred education by Library centred, child-centred education ; and
4. Replacement of service and competitive outlook by the spirit of team-work and relay work among students. This should be so extended to the University level that teachers and librarians become partners, in order to maximise the productivity of education.

REFERENCES

Sen, N.B. (ed.) ; Progress of Libraries in Free India, New Delhi, New Book Society of India, 1967.

... Madurai University Library, 10th Anniversary Souvenir, 14th Dec., 1968.

Reddy, D.J. ; Challenges in Higher Education, S.V. University, Tirupati, 1972.

UGC. New Delhi ; Report on University and College Libraries, New Delhi, UGC, 1965.

Roe, Ernest ; Teachers, Librarians and Children, London, Crosby Lockwood & Son Ltd., 1966.

Ranganathan, S.R. ; Manual of Reference Service, Bombay, Asia Publishing House, 1966.

LIBRARIANSHIP

Library Science Education in India

During the past hundred years of Library Science Education, many significant developments have taken place and this placed the librarianship in a reputed position. India's contribution to the field of library science is singularly significant. It has produced a genius in the person of Dr. S.R. Ranganathan who was adored as father of library science in India. His contributions to the subject, placed India prominently in the world map of Library Science. His enunciation of Five Laws of Library Science ; design of Colon Classification ; Classified Catalogue Code ; Chain Indexing and his Classic works, viz. Prolegomenon to Library Classification ; "Headings and Canons" ; gave India a respectable and enduring place in the world of Librarianship.

Before 1950, there were only six university schools of Library Science offering course in Librarianship. Today, the subject is offered in more than 50 universities, out of which 20 are offering M.L.I.Sc. Course. Today, the annual output of students in B.L.I. Sc. are about 2000 and 200 in M.L.I.Sc., besides 25 students provided by D.R.T.C. and INSDOC put together. This is a bright picture of the development of Library and Information Science Schools. It is to be noted that today, admission into the courses are in much demand, as there is high potentiality in employment market. Thus, there is much competition for admission into these courses and bright students are being attracted.

Library Science degrees and departments are now renamed as Library and Information Science degrees and departments. This indicates the development and enhanced scope of this subject. It also reveals the response to the changing demands on Library Science Education and Library Services.

Profs. Neelameghan, Mangla, Isaac, Girja Kumar, Kaula and many others, have made elaborate studies on Library Science Education in India. They have emphasised the need of Library Education in various Committees, Conferences, Seminars and recommendations were made towards the design and development of library science education in India. So, here, I only wish to present some of my views on this subject.

According to Whitehead "Education is the acquisition of the art of utilisation of knowledge". This implies that the responsibility of the Student is to learn rather than to be taught. Therefore, Library Science teacher should teach the Student the basic elements of the subject that make the student to learn himself and further explore the subject. Library Science, though developed its own theory in earlier times, yet. in the application, it largely depends upon other disciplines. Hence a student of library science should be made to understand this peculiar nature of the subject and make the student always learn about other basic disciplines as well. He cannot classify a book by simply using the Classification Schedule. He should be able to understand the subject of the book and genesis of subject, then only he can classify it, similarly he cannot assign subject headings without some understanding of the subject. That is why a Librarian or Library Science Student, should continuously be a learner or student. This will keep him in good command not only as a librarian, but as an academician.

Certificate (C.L. Sc.), Bachelors (B.L.I.Sc.), Master (M.L.I.Sc. M. Phil, Ph. D. Associateship are the different levels of course in Library Science available in our country. Long back, it has been decided that C.L.Sc. Course be taken away from the scope of University Library Science Departments and be entrusted to State level library Associations or any other Library Organisations or to the Department of Public Libraries to run the teaching courses. But still it is offered by some Universities. More so, in our own University, the Institute of Correspondence Courses is offering C.L.I.Sc. Course by Correspondence in both English and Telugu mediums. The admissions are made purely on merit, basing on the marks obtained in Intermediate Course (Plus two system). The course is of six month's duration and the students are required to attend contact classes for ten days after four month's learning. Lessons are prepared by the Staff of the University Library and Department. This Course is satisfying the employment domand for the personnel to man local libraries and with Junior Positions in other academic and special libraries.

The Andhra Pradesh Open University with its headquarters at Hyderabad, also is now running a Second batch of B.L.I.Sc. Course by Opening Study Centres at Tirupati, Vijayawada, Hyderabad, Bangalore, Vizag, Warangal and Madras under the supervision of a Coordinator appointed by APOU. The Course is of one academic year and it is open to those who have put in some experience in libraries. The students are supplied with printed lessons in all papers written by Course writers and classes are held every second Saturday and following Sunday. Attendance is not compulsory except for the ten days Summer School at the end of the course during which, Senior teachers in Library Science and Librarians from different Universities in the State will deliver lectures to the students. It is posing an issue that this type of open University Course may bring down the standards ineffectively of the Course and performance of the Student. In this Course we have to avail and see how much students learn the practical aspects of the subjects like Classification, Cataloguing, Reference Service, Bibliography etc. I am not against the system with regard to the Open Universities, but it is lacking facilities for the students who should be made to attend classes for a minimum period of 15 days' duration of Contact Classes and during this period students should be taught the practical aspects of the above mentioned subjects, besides theory oriented Book Selection. Subjects like library organisation, and administration.

The Andhra Pradesh State Government have also instituted Telugu Academy with its headquarters at Hyderabad to bring out Text books in the Intermediate (Plus Two System) and degree levels in the regional language of Telugu. The B.L.I.Sc. degree Course materials preparation was also taken up by the Telugu Academy by appointing Course Writers and Editors for each Text book from among the specialists and Experts in the Subjects of the Library Science faculties of Andhra Pradesh. It is expected of the Telugu Academy authorities to take substantive steps in expediting the work of course writers and editors of the respective subjects in library science by removing certain slugs on the way and complete the same soon for the use of the students of library and Information Science Schools to those who opted for Telugu as their medium. Similar course material in Library Science is also being produced in the Hindi language by the North Indians. The Library Science Course material in various Indian Languages publishing is a good sign to understand the subjects in their own mother tongue better and by many.

As already mentioned, Library Science as a discipline in practice has to depend upon other disciplines as well. For example, Bibliometrics can be taught well with some specialisation of Mathematic Statistics background. Similarly, computer applications can be taught only after some specialised training and to some with basic knowledge of Mathematics. To teach Indexing, knowledge of the subject is essential. So, a Library Science department would be well, if it has on its staff, with different basic subject background, and specialised training in computer applications in libraries. Thus Library Science teachers even if they do not have specialisation like the one above mentioned, facility should be made available to undergo such in-service training to teach such subjects effectively. Also, there is need for training in the teaching techniques. Hence, a developed library school with all infrastructural facilities, is to be identified and entrusted with giving training in the teaching techniques in Library Science. This is one of the important recommendations made by many Seminars on this subject. Wherever, M. Phil and Ph. D. are available, they should get preference in the recruitment of teachers. Facilities should be made available for part time research and Faculty improvement programme, as available in other disciplines for obtaining the M. Phil and Ph. D. qualifications by the teachers, should be emphasised. Recently there is a sudden spurt of doctorates in Library Science in India and it is a welcome sign.

Students admitted to library Science courses should be selected from all the disciplines viz., Humanities, Social Sciences, Physical and Biological Science ; otherwise, there will be a shortage of personnel required in special libraries, requiring particular subject background. Most of the employment potentiality is in the Science and Technology Library and Information Centres. They require only candidates with Physical Sciences background. In such cases, Library Schools should not be in short supply of such candidates. Students should be impressed that they should obtain a basic knowledge of different disciplines and should be taught the technique of how to learn or get familiarity with the contents of different disciplines. The techniques may be to study Classification schedules, or in evaluating Encyclopaedias etc. Also, the Students should be impressed of changing demands of the profession and that they should learn computer applications with interest.

It has been recommended that a Library Science student should undergo 3 to 4 months pre-admission apprenticeship, for admission to B.L.I.Sc. and one or two years' experience for admission to M.L.I.Sc. Course.

Classification Schedules are in short supply and high priced. Effort; need to be made that these are available in required number and also the copies of the same should be made available at reasonable cost to be purchased by the librarians once they enter the job.

It will not be out of context, to mention that Colon Classification 7th edition, will soon be available in enough copies for purchase by the library schools and librarians. Similarly, Dictionary Catalogue Code of S.R. Ranganathan and Anglo-American Cataloguing Rules also be made available in Indian edition at reasonable cost. Many of Ranganathan's books are now out of stock and not available even in the old libraries. Arrangements need to be made to bring out reprints or new editions of these books.

Library Science literature, especially, text books, in regional languages need to be produced. Library Associations should take the lead in this direction with Government and Library Schools. There is shortage of Indian Reference Sources especially of Indian topics in Encyclopaedias. It is also the responsibility of library profession to compile such reference sources. There is a shortage of text books suitable for use in Indian Library Schools relevant to Indian conditions.

Organisations like UGC, DST, ICSSR, ILA, IASLIC, UNESCO have a greater role to play in extending support for research and training in library and information science and equip the library personnel with new trends and developments in the field and evolve the younger generation of librarians and to see that library Information Centres serve the user community effectively.

The UGC with visiting Fellow/Lecturer/Professor Scheme makes it possible for inviting senior teachers to schools which can avail their expertise. This kind of programmes should be extended liberally in more schools.

IATLIS is now issuing a newsletter. It should convert into a Journal, so that a separate Journal of Teachers of Indian Library and Information Science Education will be avilable.

Librarians and Library Science teachers are able to visit developed countries like U.K., U.S.A., and G.D.R. under cultural exchange programme and on Commonwealth teacher fellowship etc., to study, participate in Library Education Programmes, Short-term Courses, Summer Institutes, Workshops. These facilities should be extended to more number of library and information science teachers and personnel.

Conclusion

To conclude with an encouraging note, library science programmes are bound to expand and widen their vistas and be effective with the changing technological environment with wide network of library schools throughout the country with the support of U.G.C., Library Associations and international bodies like UNESCO, FID, IFLA.

As a caution, it should be stated that, there should be an integration between library personnel and Information personnel and no scope should be given for dichotomy.

Added to this, the UGC which is looking after the working of the Academic Libraries in higher learning (University and College) and the Library Science teachers in the various Schools of Library and Information Science in the country have given the Status and salaries on par with any other faculty members. I may also be permitted to add here the fact that recently Andhra Pradesh Government has redesignated the existing cadre of College Librarians as Lecturers in Library Science.

The Schools of Library and Information Science in the country should concentrate upon establishing a working laboratory for the library department after designing a model so that each school can institute the same so as to be used by the students and teachers as well. These laboratories should evolve new systems and simplify indexing, Abstracting Services, prepare Bibliographies, use Audio-Visual materials and Video Cassettes of the programme as teaching aids.

CIRCULATION SYSTEMS
To Meet User's Need

The circulation function in libraries involves every user of library materials and the successful performance of the function is a measure of the effectiveness of all other duties to which librarians devote themselves. The best equipped library, located in the most modern university, and staffed with the most capable librarians, would be a mausoleum of recorded knowledge if the circulation function were omitted. The processes and services which result in bringing users and the library materials into productive relationship are circulation functions in libraries. Obviously, a library user must have access to material before he can make use of it at all, but given access, the library material must be what he needs before the relationship between user and material can be productive. The fact that a library user's request is fulfilled can be sterile achievement unless at the same time, he gets what he can use to personal advantage for his current need.

Today, the educational and recreational potentialities of libraries are greater than they have ever been. While libraries are stocked with literally millions of books and other resources, the ultimate goal—their use—is only partially achieved.

In the past, circulation service was the sole reader service. Inherent in the situation was the opportunity for the librarian to know the borrower's need. The librarian also knew its resources, and was thus able to fulfil the need within the limits of materials available and of his own competence.

During the past century, the concept of the circulation function has changed radically. Circulation services were first departmentalised and subsequently were decentralised. A de-emphasis of reader services, or an emphasis on the personal resourcefulness of the user, has occurred during a period when the sources of information in libraries increased enormously in quantity and form, but also during a period when the successful retrieval of information grew increasingly more dependent upon technical skill. In all sincerity and through a sense of obligation in a scientific age, librarians have used machines to replace critical manpower, speed up processes, and reduce unit costs. Faced with acute shortages of professional personnel, librarians have conscientiously replaced professional with clerical personnel in identifiable clerical operations. The circulation function was both favourably and adversely affected by progressive administrators. It is now symbolized by the charging machine, and the reader services, formerly an integral part of the circulation function, are gone. Most important is the loss of control over the effective use of library materials.

The circulation department's primary function is to supply the library user the books, pamphlets, serials, and other materials wanted. Four major funtions comprise circulation work : the staff must have a familiarity with the holdings of the library, a knowledge of the needs and interests of the users, appreciation the techniques employed in carrying out the service policies of the institution, and a willingness to cooperate with the other departments of the library.

In many respects, the circulation desk is the library's reception room as well as its book distribution and information centre. Indeed, the users frequently judge the library and its administration by the general atmosphere and level of service at the circulation desk. It is curious that, despite its nerve centre role, the circulation desk has been accorded relatively little attention by writers on library techniques. The lack of information regarding the service requirements of students and faculty members in colleges and universities has been noted.

The circulation department, being responsible for loan services, usually maintains a record of all loans ; keeps a file of registered borrowers ; provides machinery for the recall of overdue items and for titles in demand ; refers to stack reference assistants in view of heavy work involved in the present days ; supervises the shelving of materials in the stacks ; and arranges extension, inter-library, and public relations services.

The organization of the circulation department depends upon the size of the library, the scope of its work, and the degree of departmentalisation. Each type of library—public, college, university, and special—has particular needs, and the organization must reflect these needs. While every circulation department must be organized to give speedy and efficient service, this goal must be regarded as a means rather than an end in itself. In the college and university, the end is to advance the instruction and research programmes ; in the special library it is to further the s.ccessful operation of the business or profession ; in the public library field (a) to facilitate informed self-education of all people in the community, (b) to enrich and further develop the subjects on which individuals are undertaking formal education, (c) to meet the information needs of all, (d) to support the educational, civil and cultural activities groups and organisations, and (e) to encourage wholesale recreation and constructive use of leisure time.

The method of lending books to members of the library for home reading seems, to a certain extent, to be the outcome of the five laws of library science advocated by the late Dr. S.R. Ranganathan. For the effective use of books available in the library and also to help the readers who may not find time to read within the library, lending of books outside the library is inevitable. This device not only promotes the reading habit outside the library but also beyond library hours. The issue of books attracts more readers to use the library. The circulation system is one kind of publicity for the books in the library. The provision of borrowing facilities prevents the overcrowding of readers in the reading room and facilitates the maintenance of the library with a limited seating capacity. The issue method gives an idea of the books widely used and less used and also the intellectual tastes of the different borrowers of the library. Thus, the circulation section is an important one, reflecting the image of the entire library.

When the libraries were not properly organized for want of adequate professional staff and suitable users, there were many crude methods of charging in the circulation systems. Many of them are still used by a few small libraries in India.

Ledger Type or Register System : Books are borrowed through the main counter, being charged and discharged by a single individual. In this system, an individual borrower is assigned one or two pages or leaves in a ledger and the transaction is noted when borrowed and returned as the case may be. An index to the borrower's name is provided to facilitate easy location for recording entries. In this register the columns are as follows :

Name of the Borrower ;

Department :

S. No.	*Author*	*Title of the book*	*Acc. No.*	*Date of issue*	*Signature of the Borrower*	*Signature of the Asst. after return with date*

Prior to the days of the literature explosion, when the borrowers were limited and books were less used, this system was held good. This system has its own advantages and disadvantages.

Advantages. (a) Highly authentic since both the borrower and the assistant in charge signs over every transaction ; (b) reveals the entire range of books borrowed and used ; (c) shows at a glance the number of books due over a period of time ; (d) the best method for small libraries.

Disadvantages. (a) Consumes more time for filling up all the columns in the register ; (b) the possibility of losing pages in the register due to constant use and wear and tear.

Library Borrower's Card System : Among the different charging systems followed in India, the library borrower's card system is used in small libraries having limited membership. This is an improvement over the ledger system mentioned earlier. This card was used during the initial stages of S.V. University library when there were limited borrowers.

This description of the card is given hereunder.

Every member of the library is provided with the borrowers card. The number of cards issued depends on the type of readers, *i.e.*, students, research scholars, faculty members, and administrative staff of various cadres. One book is issued against one card. The reader intending to borrow a book must present the book and the borrower card at the issue counter after filling out the accession number and call number of the required book with his initials. The concerned assistant, after verification of the entries in the card with the book, puts his initials in the card against the entry, and issues the book to

Front View of the Card
Size : 15 cm ✕ 10 cm

S.V. UNIVERSITY LIBRARY, TIRUPATI
LIBRARY BORROWERS CARD

Expires————

No.————
Name——————————————————
Class——————————————Group——————————
Signature of the Borrower : ——————————————————————

Acc. No.	*Call No.*	*Borrower's initials and Date*	*Initials of the Assistant*	*Date of Return*	*Initials of the Assistant*

Back View of the Card

Acc. No.	*Call No.*	*Borrower's initials and Date*	*Initials of the Assistant*	*Date of Return*	*Initals of the Assistant*

the reader after putting the due date over the date label posted inside the book. The charged card is then arranged in the serial order of the borrower's number in the charging tray. When the book is returned by the borrower, the concerned assistant at the return desk picks out the card arranged in the charging tray and returns the card to the borrower after verification with the book returned.

Advantages. (a) The borrower's card is the record of all the books issued to and returned by a particular borrower with details of the date of issue and return.

(b) The time required for charging and discharging books under this system is less compared to the ledger system, where pages allotted to the respective borrowers have to be turned every time for recording the issue and return transactions.

(c) The possibility of misusing the card by another person is eliminated since the difference in signature can be identified.

(d) The reader is also assured of the correctness of the transaction dealing with the issue and return of books, since the books are issued only on the basis of his initials.

(e) The card gives the idea of the nature of the books used by a particular reader.

(f) Wrong charging of book is avoided.

Disadvantages. (a) This system is not helpful in a big library with heavy circulation of books.

(b) It is time-consuming and quick issue and return of books is not possible under this system, compared to the Browne system.

(c) The loss of a charged card means the loss of the book charged under that card.

(d) Information as to whom the particular book was issued may not be possible, since the cards are arranged in serial order of the borrowers.

(e) In light of the merits and demerits of this system, the borrower's card system is best suited for adoption in small libraries with a limited number of borrowers.

The Browne and Newark Systems

The Browne and Newark systems are not discussed here, since they are already in vogue in Indian libraries. With the increase in issue and return transactions in the library caused by growth in library membership, the borrower's card system was found unsuitable in this situation. To save the reader and staff, the Browne system of charging was introduced to expedite the transactions. This system not only facilitated the quick issue and return of books but also enabled the library to furnish the information about when and by whom the book required by another person was borrowed. The system works very well in practice in spite of the fact that it gives scope of misuse and wrong charging of books. To overcome this defect and to make the Browne system function properly, the pass-book system was introduced. For every borrower a passbook is issued along with the borrower's tickets. The passbook, in addition to the columns mentioned below, contains the passport-size photograph of the borrower and the borrower's name, office address, and residential address.

SAMPLE

PASSPORT SIZE PHOTO	Register No. ____ Name of the Borrower : ____ ____ Address ____ ____ Residential Address : ____ ____

Acc. No.	*Call No.*	*Borrower's initial with date*	*Initials of Asst. at the issue counter with date*	*Initials of Asst. at return counter with date*

Introduction of the passbook to supplement the Browne system provides a record of the books borrowed and returned by a particular borrower with dates of issues and returns. The entries have to be made in the passbook by the member and present the same to the counter assistant in person, along with the charging ticket at the time of borrowing the book. When returning the book, the counter assistant takes out the charged ticket and the passbook of the borrower. After noting the date of return with initials for the book received for return in the presence of the borrower, the counter assistant returns the borrower's ticket after putting back the passbook in the serial order of the borrowers of the library. The passbook prevents the misuse of tickets by persons other than borrowers and also acts as a check over sublending of tickets. The passbook is not returned to the borrower but is kept under the custody of the counter assistant.

This system, which is an improvement over the Browne system, furnishes the record of books taken and returned by a particular borrower with the help of passbook. The entries in the passbook also reveal much statistical information : number of books borrowed, nature of books borrowed, number of times borrowed, etc. Furthermore, the information about the issue of a particular book or books can be found by going through borrowers' tickets arranged in a classified date order.

In view of the above facts, the system under discussion is best suited for adoption in Indian libraries under the present conditions, although more time is involved in charging and discharging of issues compared to the Browne system.

Although there are many other circulation systems available, including an automated circulation system which has many advantages over the manual or mechanical systems, most college and university or public and special libraries in India cannot afford to buy the systems. Nor are they ready for the system due to the size of their libraries. Only big university libraries such as Delhi, Bombay, Calcutta, or Madras can buy this system or even have on-line circulation systems in their libraries. On-line systems such as Gaylord and others are being used successfully in the United States. The consideration in choosing any circulation system is that it should not be complicated. It should be easy to use, inexpensive, efficient, and should meet the needs of an institution.

REFERENCES

Adelabau, A. "Some Thoughts on Book Circulation in University Libraries." *Nigerian Librarian*, 9 (1973), 75-81.

Buckland, M.K. *Book Availability and the Library User*. New York : Pergamon, 1975.

Burgess, T.K. "Cost Effectiveness Model for Comparing Various Circulation Systems." *Journal of Library Automation*, 6 (1973), 75-86.

Christopher, H.G.T. "Dickman Book Charging System." *Library World*, 39 (1937), 231-236.

"Circulation Work." In G.R. Lyle, *Administration of the College Library*. 4th ed. New York ; H.W. Wilson, 1974, pp. 68-69.

Clarke, R.F., and Clarke, H.G. "Your Charging System : Is It Thief Proof ?" *Library Journal*, 91 (1966), 642-643.

Dennis, D.D., and Stockton, P.A. "Automated Library Circulation System Boosts Services Control at American University." *Special Libraries*, 65 (1974), 512-515.

Elliott, C.A. "Islington Book Charging System." *Library Association Record* 67 (1965), 58-59.

Haber, W. "Gaylord Charging : Big Circulation—Think Small," *Unabashed Librarian*, 10 (Winter 1974), 5.

Hardesty. L. "Academic Library : Unused and Unneeded ?" *Library Scene*, 4 (Dec. 1975-Mar. 1976), 14-16.

Hood, M.J., and Lyle, G.R. "New System of Book Charging for College Libraries." *Library Journal*, 65 (1940). 18-20.

Hunt. D.H., ed. "Charging Sytems." *Drexel Library Quarterly*, 1 (1965), 1-37.

Jenks, G.M. "Circulation and Its Relationship to the Book Collection and Academic Departments." *College & Research Libraries*, 37 (1976), 145-52.

Kilgur, F.G. "New Punched Cards for Circulation Records." *Library Journcl*, 64 (1939), 131-133.

Lehman, B.M. "Comparison of Non-manual Charging Systems in Libraries" Master's thesis, Pratt Institute Library School, 1952.

Lin, S.H. "Edinboro Automated Circulation System." *Network*, 3 (Spring 1976), 6-19.

Lucy, E. "Circulation System to Consider." *Ontario Library Review*, 48 (1964), 86-90.

McGaw, H.F. "Self-Charging System." *Wilson Library Bulletin*, 16 (1942), 658-660.

McKendrick, S. University of Sydney Library's On-Line Circulation System : A Workshop Case Study." *LASIE*, 6 (1975), 35-54.

McKibbin, D. "On-Line Circulation Control : Three Years Experience." *Canadian Library Journal*, 31 (1974), 214-216 ff.

Miller, L.A. "Role of Circulation Services in the Major University Library." *College & Research Libraries*' 34 (1973), 463-471.

Sandall, F.A. "Simple Triple Entry Charging Scheme." *New Zealand Libraries*, 2 (1939), 47-48.

Shanbhogue, K.G. "Compromise in the System of Issue or Charging and Discharging of Books." *Herald of Library Science*, 4 (1965), 169-170.

Smith, C.E. "Token Charging with Controls." *Australian Library Journal*, 25 (1976), 22-25.

Trueswell, R.W. "Two Characteristics of Circulation and Their Effect on the Implementation of Mechanized Circulation Control System." *College & Research Libraries*, 25 (1964), 285-291.

Young, B. "Circulation Services : Is It Meeting the User's Needs ?" *Journal of Academic Librarianship*, 2 (1976). 120-125.

ACADEMIC LIBRARY
Education Through Audio-Visual Aids

The importance of educating the library user in how to make the the fullest possible use of the facilities available to them, in achieving this, the emphasis on self-education and use of tutorials in higher education increased. The need for such user instruction and action taken to overcome the communications barrier between the user and the documents to some extent appreciable.

There has been growing interest in modern Academic and special libraries for user instruction through the developments in information new technology, use of computers and Audio-Visual Aids for the effective use of libraries and for evaluation in a user education programme in Higher Education. I may be permitted to quote here useful information which will be appropriate on this topic.

This aspect of Audio-Visual through user education is a spirit of enterprise-which is nothing but an incessant human striving for a better life to keep abreast with the changing situations to face the challenges with determination.

Human history is an endless relay race in which the baton of life is handed over from one generation to another. It is a continuing challenge to transmit life to future generations. So long as this chain of life stays viable on earth, the 'spirit of enterprise' will continue to enlighten humanity.

The life of an individual is short and transient and one's sphere of activities is hunted by both temporal and spatial boundaries. Without this short span of life, as so much can be intended from the past and imparted to the future. Thus, the most significant mission intended to each human being is the act as a transmitter be selecting from the enormous historical and cultural inheritance of the past, the richest as such of mankind to be passed down to future generations.

We are approaching the dawn of 21st Century. Technological advancements have brought tremendous progress industrializing a very small part of this world. But, on the other hand, the great part of the world is still unable to face its peoples for the threats of poverty, hunger and depletion of natural resources, as well as the natural and cultural disruption of the environment. Our globe is now equipped with the potential capabilities of self-disruption. We are also exposed to the fear of war. Today, the spirit of enterprise is needed more than ever before to eliminate the source of fear and to bring prosperity to the proven majority suffering from daily wants.

What is pressingly needed today is the perception to shape humanity into a peaceful community. If the wisdom, foresight and dedication revealed by the community are fully employed to create a better world, then we can be optimistic for the future freedom, peace and happiness of all mankind.

(1) "Make use of your Library, to be enlightened and entertained. To be a well informed citizen. To achieve academic distinction and to win a life-time of good reading."

(2) "It is well for us to realise that the great increase in knowledge in the world does not necessarily make us better or wiser. We must know how to use the knowledge properly before we can fully profit by it." So goes a sign-board displayed at the entrance in some of our academic libraries.

Frederic Mayer, the great American educator, had the same idea in mind when he stated.

"If they (the students) learn to love books their entire existence will change. As persons they will have deeper insights. Old age will lose part of its terror and time will be something purely phenomenal. Distance will have no meaning and the past will be as intriguing as the future and they will never be alone even in times of illness and despair. To love books is to see the ideal possibilities of humanity."

It is clear from the above that the most important aim of higher education is not merely the great increase in knowledge, bagging of academic distinctions and the winning of laurels and gold medals, but the weaving into the very tapestry of one's life a liking for good books and a never-quenching thirst for judicious and selective reading.

In all types of libraries, documentation centres/information centres there is an enormous wastage of library resources due to non-use of them properly by their readers. With shrinking budgets, the libraries must encourage users to make greater use of available resources. Educating the user is the proper solution for the librarians and pioneers in the field. Educating the library user improves the quality of use. User education aims to provide knowledge and skills necessary for a user to find out his own way. User Education in recent years has become the subject of a great deal of activity and concern in western countries. It has caught the imagination of professional libraians all over the world. The name of Louis Shores, Patricia B. Knapp and Thomas G. Kirk are worth mentioning on this occasion since these names are recorded as land-marks in the annals of User Education.

In India, User Education is beginning to get more attention. The INSDOC (New Delhi), DRIC (Bangalore) and IASLIC have organised some activity by promoting seminars and workshops. There is complete lack of teaching aids including written and audio-visual ones required for user educational programmes to serve Indian requirements. Mention deserve to be made about instructional tape/slide kit entitled 'Let us find out' produced by INSDOC. It was prepared for the school going children for use of libraries. There is a need for more such kits to meet different kinds of requirements.

An Academic/Research Library, however, great its contents are and grand its facilities, is not an end in itself. It should be like a flower garden in its well being, so that the creative minds are attracted to it. To achieve this, there should be commendable cooperation and willingness to help from the library staff. With an over all air of 'human touch' in their various functions, after all in library science, the user is the vital-link, is it not ? Reputed Scientists/Researchers should cultivate the norm of acknowledging the library which they used for their research activities ; Computers are given such credit nowadays. Do libraries not deserve so ? A close liaison between any research project team and the supporting library is essential. The library can also act as the reader to be on the look out to update the research team on the day-to-day basis about similar or allied activities done by others ; this helps in avoiding the duplication of efforts and reinventing the old things.

A well organised Academic/Research library should orient itself and help the researcher to scan the information and come to conclusions with minimum efforts ; otherwise details heaped before him and will be a drifting wood caught up in the turbulent communication currents. At the best, any library is like a torch-light and it is mostly left to the researcher how well he should handle it during the exploration.

In the light of the above background how best a librarian can come to the rescue of the users for rendering service through education Audio-visual teaching aids of the library resources has to be discussed here.

(1) A general orientation to available facilities and resources.

(2) The teaching of basic research skills and strategies.

(3) The teaching of the organisation of the literature in various disciplines as well as the basic reference tools in each discipline. These objectives will assist the users to acquire skills for effective application information retrieval through user education.

Orientation Programme

The problem of inefficient use of libraries led to the introduction of 'Reference Service' in academic libraries in the late 1880s in U.S.A as a first step to improve the use of libraries. The tedium of answering the same questions again and again might have led to the development of orientation programmes.

An orientation programme aims at acquainting the freshman with some of the basics concerning the library use. Orientation is "Concerned with introducing the user to the general Techniques of library usages and services available in library and, in particular, to the organization, services and layout of a particular library." It is intended "(a) to familiarise users with the physical layout and the procedures for using the library units relevant to their needs. (b) To make users aware of the staff that is available to assist them and to make users comfortable in seeking assistance. (c) To inform users about basic library holdings, record such as the card catalogue and serials list that can be used to locate materials within the system." Thus orientation is concerned with introducing the users to the library if possible physically or through Audio-Visual teaching aids so that they become aware of physical location of different sections, staff collection and services. Dr. S.R. Ranganathan has enunciated the use of the term initiation and of a freshman instead of orientation.

I shall now concern myself with describing how the programme can be conducted through Audio-visual aids for user instruction on the campuses of Academic libraries. In a lecture programme, it can also be exhibited or screened through Audios, depicting the way the College Library is organised and how to make use of the Resources of the library, how the scheme of classification bring like books together, how the reference books are all-yielding so far as information is concerned, how the circulation of books section performs its job. The lecture (film show) could be sand-wiched in between film and slide show depicting the working of well established libraries etc. Tape-slide programme or 20 minutes on finding information, sources or information, using literature search. Audio-cassette programme of 15 minutes on how to use Arts and Humanities Citation Index to be used in conjunction with the Index. The film and slide shows will have an enduring impact on the minds of the school and College and University Library Users itself.

Films like library ; Morning, Noon and Night ; the National Library of India ; the Library of Congress ; Books for all ; in addition to relieving the monotony of the lecture method programmes like, Quiz, Symposia, Seminars and Conferences, Book Exhibitions, Library automation services, etc., and enliven the minds of the listeners by the edifying spectacle they show of grand libraries, the spirit, background music etc.

The quote, I may mention here that Sri Venkateswara Univesity Library at Tirupati, is possessing educative films (16mm and 35mm) on various subjects, for British open University, U.K., Film project T.V. slides and slide projector, V.C.P. (Video Cassette Player) Microfilms and Microfiche, equipments like Microfilm Reader and intercom phone facility provided for each section within the library also. Further, the reprographic equipment like plain paper copier for the use of the Library users. We are contemplating on to provide a separate hall in the University Library with 120 seating arrangements and Film Library equipment storage room at an early date. Experience has shown us the use of Audio-visual material will be much useful to attract the users and to develop reading habit in the library in a well furnished accommodation, ventilation, lighting and cool air facilities according to our Indian climatic conditions.

User Education consists of four inter-related components, user awareness : Library orientation, interest profiling and bibliographic instruction. The concept of Library use instruction programme is defined "as a procedure whereby students are taught to use Library devices such as the Card Catalogue, Bibliographical tools, basic reference tools, primary sources of documents periodical indexes, subject reference sources etc. and to utilize effective search strategies in the Library."

The proliferation of all the world literatures cannot find place in the Academic libraries for acquisition. Library material can be selected on the basis of book selection principles. With developments in user education, methods of instruction have changed and become more varied. However, it has been found that there is no single method or media, which could serve as a panacea for all the categories of user education programmes. There are three types of teaching methods viz. (a) Those suitable for group instruction, (b) Those suitable for individual instruction, (c) Ones suitable for both individual and group instruction. Choice of teaching methods and media depends upon learning teaching situation, the students and teachers and subject material available for the purpose and experience has shown that no single method can be suitable for all situations.

The design of modular system of library use instruction each modula available to any user at the place of need, at any time the library was open can be used. Using MIT Barker engineering library as a laboratory, the model library staff has developed a series or short audio-visual programmes, each one discussing one reference source, such as Engineering Index or Science citation Index. The programmes vary from two to ten minutes each, designed for simple, on demand use. Each was located on a shelf next to the reference source discussed, users were provided library instruction at the time and place of actual need. Group reader profits from the basis of such programmes.

For providing instruction, a variety of teaching aids are employed. A variety of media and equipment can be utilised for the purpose. Out of which audio-visual (slides, tape/slide, Video tape. V.C.R., T.V., films, audio tapes etc.) aids are nowadays most popular in the western countries but in India some of the University Libraries and Research and Special Libraries are using them. A variety of media and equipment may be utilised as point of the use instructional aids in the library to provide users with basic bibliographic instruction on frequently used tools which require repetitive instruction of user by librarian.

Microform took its first faltering step with the "Microscopic photographs" produced by Jhon Benjamen Dance in 1839 in

Microtechnology. Microform and user awareness of the potentiality of microform-led to an out of micropublishers who brought out microform products of primary and secondary literature. The developments in microphotography also give rise of the establishment of international standards. The formats being microform (8mm, 16mm and 35mm) Microfiche, opaque cards, etc, and the type of photos being deizo, vasicular and silver halids negative and positive. This step resulted in the genesis and perpetuation of the concept of serials storage and management in microform. In recent years, mostly American and European libraries store a sizeable portion of their correction-Journals (Primary and Secondary, back volumes and current subscriptions) theses, reports, patents standards etc. in microform. The latest developments in micro-technology relate to computerized microform (COM) management despite its praiseworthy success in Europe and America microform it is still at a very incipient stage in India. Microform is advantageous because :

1. Microform saves space.
2. Microform reduces staff time.
3. Microform slashes costs.
4. Microform has file integriate.
5. Microform is never "out of print".

Keeping in view the user's demand, frequency of use microfilming would take care of a lot of problems as noted below in seriatum :

1. In the Indian Universities, graduate students are very much examination-oriented, and it has been noticed that there is a great demand for question paper of earlier years.
2. Most librarians know the difficulties faced by not being able to provide sufficient copies of text books which have gone out of print, but continue to be on the syllabi. The non-availability creates a scarcity mentality which is greatly responsible for the mutilation and pilferage of books.

   Microfiche copies of some text books and incomplete sets of ephemeral publication can at least ensure availability.
3. Scientific and Technical reports, Census reports, Government reports, Reference works Library, Catalogues and preservation or Archival material and fragile manuscripts, data services which need constant updating, theses and

dissertations which in majority of cases do not get published, rare books, documents containing new information not previously published for sale or distribution (journals and books) newspapers etc., can be brought out through Micropublications for the benefit of users of the library.

4. Inter-Library Loan system accepted by the participating Libraries either to lend or to borrow, the postal expenses and transporting bulky volumes, Ph.D. theses etc., becomes a great barrier to information flow, with the introduction of Micoform service, we can overcome these barriers.

This Seminar was organised by Sri Venkateswara University Library, Tirupati during August 11-13, 1984. Prof. K.S. Deshpande in his keynote address at the Seminar has rightly pointed out and made a comparative study on the usage of Microforms, with well established libraries in U.K. and U.S.A. and expressed his views that our Indian Libraries have still to grow and go a long way in this direction to be successful by making more liberal financial provisions. He also mentioned about a deliberate policy of acquiring and using microforms and of whole hearted resource-sharing will certainly make even our existing meagre resources go a long way. This way our libraries will get richer and become more responsive than ever before provided our libraries faithfully implement the first four laws of library science, their pace of development needs to be monitored and regulated. Fruitful discussions were made on the topic and on its different facets. This seminar really inspired and paved the way for the participants to think seriously pros and cons for the use of Microforms in their respective libraries as a measure of providing facilities to their library users—more so to save the valuable shelf space : to reduce the cost of construction which are becoming dearer and dearer : to reduce the area of the Library building to a viable limit to save the time of the reader : and lastly to save the life of the rare and valuable collection from the claws of climatic conditions and pests that spirit the documents.

Allied UMI conducts short programmes on Microform to disabuse the faulty notions in the mind of the users and administrators about microform. These programmes are designed to make the user population more amenable to a microform collection in their Library.

The following salient constraints compel the Indian Libraries to defer the microform decision.

(a) The restrictions imposed by the government of India on the import of microform readers and related equipment, and the non-availability of good Indian readers and equipment is a major handicap for microform collection development in Indian Libraries.

(b) The present vagueness in the minds of many Indian libraries about microform management systems.

(c) The Preconceived erroneous notions of Indian users about the ill-effects of microform on the human eye, coupled with a natural tendency to repel instructions on an existing familiar frame work.

UMI (University Microfilms International) of USA offers its information products and services (mainly in microform) to Libraries and individuals, the world over. UMI welcome the Indian librarian to acquire its software as well as helps him to overcome constraints to microform purchase, in collaboration with its exclusive Agent, Allied Publishers.

UMI offers full-text copies of, and access services, to its products—much in demand out of print books (Paper and microform)—Dissertations published since 1861, backfiles and current subscriptions of over 13,000 reputed serials (Microform only) and famous Research Collections such as India Office Records and Society of Petroleum Engineers (in microform only).

This software helps the librarian to devleop a collection, reduce cost as well as provide his users with a sizeable amount of relevant information.

Normally, user education might be considered 'a means of breaking vicious circle whereby Libraries justify the costs of services and materials in the face of no demand while users cannot demand what they do not know about, with this background IASLIC has adopted a definition for user education which includes teaching library literacy and giving instructions for bibliographic searches.

According to Ruth Alston, as a result of her analysis she had drawn certain conclusions some of which are worth mentioning here. These include :

(a) 'It appears that despite NISSAT, the information profession had in fact truly failed to convince the Central Government that information is an essential part of nation's resources and that any development plan which does not incorporate the fullest provision is mere myopia'.

(b) 'Considering the available resources and needs very little Inter Library Loan (ILL) exists and even if it exists it operates mostly on the basis of personal contacts.

(c) The whole field of information provision relies on few dynamic librarian's enthusiasm which is not a happy situation.

(d) "The Information community in India must exert their professional skills in such a manner that the Central Government can hear their voice aimed the clamour of other competitors".

The above analysis would be considered just like a warning bell to wake up from slumber—which is the Librarian's job.

Both Librarians and educators, nowadays generally recognize that user education is a necessity and a must if libraries are to be used in an effective manner. Since the College and School Libraries are yet to be developed, the orientation programmes regarding better utilization of their limited resources through Audio-Visual teaching aids will go a long way for the support of the user education programmes. In our country like India sound user education programmes need to be developed, which are strong both on techniques and methodology. Financial resources are meagre and the changed attitude of the user community of any library should come forward and demand for the usual and normal facilities to be required from their respective authorities. The well-trained staff of any library should always be prepared to face the challenges of higher education and try to satisfy with the available information and improvising with the services that are needed by the users, thereby the Academic Libraries in particular will prosper with the sound user education programmes. The activity of Bibliographical search, referring Abstracts and Indexes in a specialised fields, list of current periodicals, Union Cotalogues, Library Card Catalogue, the Schemes of Classification and Catalogue system, location of required material, Inter Library Loan Abstracting, Indexing, Translation services, etc. will be called as user education programmes conducted by an effective librarian for the benefit of research scholars, faculty members and other users of the Library. This may also be explained to the users through using A.V.A., Microforms and other services. Any programme pertaining to user education that has to be introduced in Academic Libraries should invariably be experimented by selecting certain good libraries and if the results are fruitful than we can think of introducing them in other libraries in a phased manner depending upon the possibilities of financial resources of a particular library so also with the Audio-Visual aids introducing in the School, College and University Libraries in India. The climatic conditions of a particular area, region should also be borne in mind prior to the implementation of A.V. Programmes.

REFERENCES

Ruth Alston : Hunger for the Poor ? Some Observations on Information Provision in India, J. Inf. Sc. G. 115 (1983).

Desh Pande, K.S. : User Orientation in College Libraries. Paper presented to Indo-U.S. Seminar held at Bangalore, July 1977 (Page 1).

Krishan Kumar : User Education in ILA Bulletin Vol. XX No. 3-4 October 1984—March 1985 (pp. 88).

Stevenson (MB) : User Education Programmes 1977. The British Library Boston Spa. p. 8.

Comprehensive Programme of User Education for the General Libraries. University of Texas at Austion. 1977 (pp. 25-6).

Wilson (TD) : Guidelines for Developing and Implementing National Plan for Training in Information Use 1980 Sec. 2.4.4.

Deshpande, K.S. : User Orientation in Coll. Libraries. Indo-US Seminar 18-22, July 1977 at Bangalore.

I.L.A. Bulletin Vol. XX No. 3-4 October 1984-March 1985 (pp. 87-90).

Gita, N.S. : Microform in India : The Role of Allied-UMI (In) Relisar Vol. 1 No. 3 (1983) p. 12-13.

'Rilisar' Vol, 1 No. d (1983) p. 14-15.

THE LIBRARY BUILDING

Role of the Librarian

Modern Library planning is analogous to Economic Planning of a country. The planning of modern Library Building should be given as much importance and emphasis as to the building up of a good stock of books. An important thing observed in the planning of library building is the seriousness with which the Chief Librarian is consulted by the architect. The three important steps in the planning are programming, preliminary planning and working drawings. The librarian's role in the planning term is that of a captain of the sports team. The code of Indian Standards Institution will help improve the relationship of the Librarian with the architect and establish that the architect should design plans on the lines suggested by the Librarian.

Modern Library Planning is analogous to Economic Planning of a country. Economic Planning is a phased programme of development of a country from the state of undeveloped to underdeveloped and underdeveloped to developed state. So also modern planning of the library building is the planned development from the ancient architectural state to modern functional development. The 20th Century sees the modern era for the development of libraries both in the building up of good stock of books and in planning of modern Library buildings. Unlike the ancient library buildings which are more of architectural than functional the modern library buildings are the combination of both architectural and functional designs. Simultaneous growth in book production and knowledge in various branches of studies with their users paved way for proper housing of books and adequate accommodation with all service functions for the readers to feel at home respectively. This resulted for the planning of modern library buildings with all adroitness for service to readers and users.

The planning of modern library building should be given as much importance and emphasis as to the building up of a good stock of books. The core of a book collection is composed of (a) comprehensive collection of standard books (classics, histories, criticisms), (b) a representative selection in the major areas of knowledge (literature, art, religion, travel, business, science, education), (c) a working collection of useful tools of reference (encyclopaedias, handbooks, bibliographies, guides). In building a library, the aim is neither completeness nor well rounded book collection but one that is custom-built for its particular community. Like-wise the modern library planning should be such as to facilitate all the service functions like (a) easy access to the building, (b) ready availability of book stock, (c) proper housing and servicing facilities for periodical files, newspapers, pamphlets, Government documents etc., (d) interior conditions ensuring the comfortable use of library materials with adequate lighting, air-conditioning, sound proofing and home-like atmosphere, (e) exterior architecture, (f) floor space, (g) proper stacks and (h) epuipment of library furniture and fittings etc. for service.

Planning of library building forms an important function of modern librarianship. While it is true that the work of the library is assessed from the nature of its contents and from the service it renders, the building, which houses the material also plays a pivotal role in providing efficient library service. An ideal library, it is said must combine both functions and design and it is in this respect that planning becomes essential.

An important thing observed here in the planning of library building is the seriousness with which the Chief Librarian is consulted by the architect. The librarian not only details the basic needs which is required by library but is also connected at every stage of development. In planning some of the big libraries, the practice is to invite competitive designs for the library building, the librarian detailing the basic requirements.

The three important steps in planning library building are programming, preliminary planning and working drawings.

Programming is to include the developing of a written statement of the philosophy, principles, requirements and limitations as prepared by the librarian. This written statement is used as the basis for collaboration between the architect and librarian in the development of the plans.

In preliminary planning, the architect prepares a graphic experience of the written programme. This visual representation of the architect's interpretation provides a basis for reaching an agreement between the architect and librarian as to the direction in which the Planning is to proceed. These steps lead to the approval of precise but preliminary drawings and specifications which can be used for preliminary cost estimates.

Working drawings and specifications are the contract documents used by buildings for the preparation of tenders and bids and for the erection of the building. Working drawings include scale plans, elevations, sections and details. Further, these drawings show architectural, structural and mechanical work. Specifications include a written description of the scope of the work, general conditions, materials and workmanship involved in the project.

Out of the three major steps as detailed above, the first step is mainly concerned with the relationship between the librarian and the architect in planning the library building and that the chief function and the role of the librarian is programming. The Librarian should bear in mind the following points before he writes a programme for the Library Building.

The Librarian should learn as much as he can about library planning from the latest books and periodical articles published on the subject. He should also learn all the details he can about the educational programme of his institution and the relation of that programme to this library. He must decide on his library philosophy—his philosophy of public service, for instance and as far as possible learn what he can of the philosophy of the institution. As a whole as it affects the library, because the Philosophy of the Library may change—change as library changes, and even without the librarian changing—and that the philosophical back of the whole institution is not necessarily unchangeable. Reading of blue-prints of various library buildings and visiting of well-planned libraries of the well-developed countries are also suggested in this connection. He having prepared himself and gathered and digested the information suggested above, he should be sure to discuss in detail the problem arising from these preliminary studies with the institutions' administrative officers, faculty members and also with his own staff, which in many cases would be very helpful. A careful study of possible sites should be made, keeping in mind other things such as the slope and direction of the land, the desirability of a central location ; students' study habits and the location of class rooms. The institution's building programme for the generation ahead must also be considered as it may alter the picture completely.

As regards the preliminary planning the consensus was that a librarian consultant should be employed at the beginning of the programming of a building if the librarian lacks building planning experience and seems unable to visualize the building needs in terms of drawings. Likewise, an architect should be ready to employ a consulting architect if he is unable to effectively translate the programme into preliminary plans. Secondly, the scale models provide a means for the architect and the librarian to visualize more accurately the adequacy of the preliminary plans in terms of the programme for the building.

The librarian and architect should feel free to consult the specialist in interior decoration for furniture requirements etc., since the manufacturers of furniture are specialists to keep their products in step with modern trends and requirements.

As regards, the working drawings for which rooms, reading halls, stack areas, running water, ventilation and electrical fittings, there should be a good understanding between the librarian and architect. In this context, it is appropriate to quote the opinion of Mrs. Bryan, an expert in the library fields as follows :

"Today we have moved from the general to the specific. Our discussions today have been directed towards an understanding between librarians and architects for new library buildings. It is obvious that some very good library buildings have been planned and built and this confines the fact that librarians and architects can work together. We also note that some unstatisfactory buildings have been planned and built, which indicates we can improve this relationship. It appears that architects and librarians are and can be humane and reasonable even about different points of view and happy solutions are possible if provision is made for normal give and take by both parties. "Successful librarians are the result of interest and co-operation not just of the librarian and the architect, but the staff, faculty and most important the staff who will work in the building when it is completed. The result can be pleasing."

The Librarian's role in the planning team is that of the captain of a sports team. The team consists of the Library Authority or the Board, the Librarian and the Architect.

In developing plans, the Librarian is responsible for the general interior arrangement, relationship of service areas ; needed reader and book capacity ; equipment requirements ; location of active and less active book collection ; planning of special service needs of the institutions and all the staff service requirements.

The Library Authority or the Board is responsible for the immediate selection of a qualified, professionally trained Librarian to direct the service planning of building ; the appointment of a strong and experienced building committee ; the appointment of a qualified architect ; the aquisition of a site with the help of both the Librarian and the architect ; the provision of adequate funds for building project if it is not endowed and the sole objective of the building project being maximum Library Service at minimum cost.

The third member of the team, the architect, is responsible to help plan the interior of the building ; to consider materials and methods of construction, to design the exterior ; to design working plans and specifications ; to advertise for bids and tenders ; to furnish the Board or the Authority of the Committee with an estimate of costs ; to prepare and let the contract (after legal award of the Board) ; and to superintend the construction.

After attaining independence, the Government of India has evinced keen interest and took suitable steps in the development of the libraries on par with the Western countries. The result was the establishment of National and State Libraries and District and Panchayat Libraries as a network in the country. Various states have passed legislation to help improve the library conditions in their respective states. As a corollary to the development of libraries, the Government has drafted Indian Standard relating to the primary elements in the designing of library buildings, fittings and furniture.

The Government of India, the State Governments, the University Grants Commission have prepared extensive schemes for the development of Library facilities and setting up of new libraries in various parts of India. Many library buildings are, therefore, being constructed and some of these are attached to universities and others are public or institutional libraries. Considerable experience has been gained by librarians in the use of these libraries under the conditions obtained in India during the last 50 years and similar experience is available in the West, especially in regard to the functional designs of libraries, library fittings and library furniture. It is found desirable that the accumulated knowledge should be utilized in the design of new libraries that are now being built so that they are functionally efficient and economical. The Indian Standards Institution code is intended to provide architectural guidance in the basic elements of design pertaining to Library building, fittings and furniture.

The Librarian with the guidance of the Indian Standards Institution code and the architect can design a functional and decorative Library Building for the users with the sole objective of the building project being maximum library service at minimum cost.

Before concluding my article, it is but appropriate to make a note of the comment made by Mr. C.A. Cutter as follows :

"The architect is the natural enemy of the Librarian"—declared C.A. Cutter before the Catskill's Conference of American Library Association in 1888 and he went on to assert that architect paid no attention to the users to which a library building was to be put. He was particularly bitter about the work of H.H. Richardson as illustrated in the Howard Memorial Library. He was promptly answered, however, by W.I. Fletcher, who drew attention to the disagreements among librarians and pointed out that the architect usually worked for a committee, or a donor, but seldom for or with the librarians, who in many cases was not appointed until after the building was completed.

The architect John L. Mauran, writing one of the early phrase for a functional approach to Library Buildings, emphasized three precepts, select the Librarian, select the architect, design the Interior first. And the architect Louis E. Jallade, writing more than thirty years later, gave as his first three principles, prepare a survey, select an architect, plan with the architect. All these precepts, or principles were discussed by a friendly and co-operative group of architects and librarians at the second Princeton Conference in 1946, when little or no evidence transpired that Cutter's better remark however true, it may have secured in 1888 had any validity today."

UNIVERSITY LIBRARIANS
Some Technical Handicaps

Libraries were once regarded merely as places where books are kept ; and knowledge, as it were, is stored. Then, stress was laid more on preserving than on using them. During the past few decades, however, the tendency has been to make the library a more active agency in the community. Progressive public, college and university libraries assist in meeting civic needs, educational and social as well as recreational. As such, the importance of the librarian can never be over-emphasised, and more so in the present-day world. The librarian holds a most responsible position as the agent between the reader and the writer.

Modern libraries require well qualified and trained librarians to control and administer libraries. Apart from professional qualifications, a modern librarian should have a knowledge of the various technical aspects of his work, connected with the maintenance, preservation etc, of books. Librarian in the present era is a philosopher, a friend and a guide.

The technical handicaps in the matter of maintenance and preservation of books in modern libraries relate to book binding ; preservation of books, manuscripts and records ; microfilming and processing. These types of work are learnt theoretically under bibliography and organisation, but practical knowledge in these fields is almost nil. Even well organised institutional libraries have not a separate bindery and the necessary staff ; and other qualified and suitable personnel for microfilming and processing ; for the preservation of books, records and manuscripts. Paucity of funds is one of the chief reasons why these technical services are not provided in our libraries. Due to lack of proper training in the above mentioned fields, librarians are handicapped—leaving the libraries to their natural decay. The mere theoretical knowldge learnt during professional training will not serve the organisation of the library. Proper organisation needs good control, skill, practical knowledge to organise and supervise the work involved. Supervision over work requires practical skill in all spheres and branches of work. For example, if a qualified librarian has to organise and control a modern library equipped with modern facilities, he needs proper and qualified staff, to operate them. These functions in the different sections have to be supervised by the administrator and controller of the library, i.e., the librarian or his deputy. Hence, the need for the librarian also to have practical training in all the above mentioned fields. It is only then that the librarian can have the capacity to control and supervise the work in the library.

Before actually suggesting remedies to overcome the technical obstacles and handicaps, let me explain briefly some of the technical handicaps faced by librarians in this country.

According to Douglass Cockrell "the book-binding and care of books is intended to supplement and not to supplant workshop training for book binders. So, one can become a skilled workman by reading text books but to a man who has acquired skill and practical experience, a text book, giving perhaps different methods from these to which he has been accustomed may be helpful". So, the mere theoretical knowledge without practical skill will not help to improve a particular field. A knowledge of the technical aspects of the work is most valuable asset to the librarian. As the proverb goes, "a stitch in time saves nine", unless the book is bound in time, it is not possible to preserve it. The question of binding is a problem to be solved by the librarian. This at times, leads to many complications. At times, the dilemma arises whether a book has to be bound as soon as it is purchased or after its use for some time when the cover becomes loose and the stitching breaks. Some libraries prefer binding of books as soon as they are purchased but some other only after they are spoiled and made shapeless. This is one of the reasons why the library prefers purchasing library editions, which are bound originally. Even this type of bound books should also be got bound after some time when they are worn out and torn. The books that are originally bound possess case binding and hence need not be bound completely because they retain cardboards intact, but require only repairs with calico and restitching.

Book binding as an art should be made familiar to the librarian. The librarian is the person in the midst of an ocean of books, and he is the proper person who can have the knowledge to say that a particular type of book requires a particular type of binding. Binding of books is not a big problem in the case of scientific and technological books and reference books like, Dictionaries, Directories and Encyclopaedias which are originally casebound according to their value, use and requirement. But it is a problem with fiction and other language books and especially with books published in India. This much discussed problem has got to be taken serious notice of both by the publishers and the librarians when alone books of lasting strength can be acquired by libraries.

During recent years, University and Research Libraries in India are purchasing thousands of books out of the grants released by the University Grants Commission. When the purchases grow, naturally the stock of books also grow proportionately, and so problems of preservation need attention.

Most of the University libraries in India do not have a bindery section of their own. Usually these libraries have contract binders to whom the binding work is entrusted. In fact, there are qualified librarians as heads of libraries but they require practical knowledge in binding work. The lack of practical knowledge in book binding and binding materials, is a drawback in calling for quotations and in supervising the work done by the contract binders. More theoretical knowledge would help in the drawing up a contract, its terms and conditions. But practical knowledge alone can help a librarian to get the work done in a proper way. Unless the librarian possesses a good knowledge in certifying the materials used, type of binding done, kind of stitching made, quality of leather or buckram used for top and spines, variety of calico used and suitable cloth and twine used for end-joints and stitching, it is not possible for him to supervise the work satisfactorily. Of course, the calling of quotation for binding work can be avoided if a bindery section is attached to the library, but yet, practical knowledge is essential even to supervise the work done by the staff of the bindery. The question of binding is to be discussed not from the point of view of its decoration and economy but from the perspective of its utility and strength and its power of resistance against constant wear and tear.

The librarian's knowledge should also extend to the proper type of binding that books require. All the books do not require the same attention. Only books that require binding should be got bound and the rest discarded and withdrawn from the stock. For example, fiction books need not be paid much attention with regard to their binding. Subject books on Sciences, Humanities and Technology, and Reference books and Manuscripts etc., should be bound precisely and according to their purpose and utility. Apart from the cost of the book, the utility and purpose of the book used, and the number of readers that use it, should be the criterion for book-binding. Even as regards back numbers of journals and periodicals, the types of binding like leather binding with gold lettering (Law-book binding), full calico binding, half-leather binding or ordinary type of binding, should each be considered on its merits before they are actually entrusted for binding.

It is appropriate to mention in this context the views of John Alden, a U.S. Librarian, with regard to the care of books in India. "Firstly in the field of the repair of damaged materials, Indian Libraries suffer (further more) in two respects. The first of these is that many of the materials found most satisfactory for repair and restoration are not available in India. The locally made products are not satisfactory. Indian Tanners are unable to prepare suitable leathers for binding and cloth manufacturers are unable to manufacture satisfactorily cloth and buckram for binding, which is also a mystery. Secondly, suitable paper is not available such as a highly cellulose content paper which can be expected to last-through once good rag papers, which have endured for centuries were made in India. No good record paper, Japanese tissue, good quality silk for repair are available.

Materials apart, there is an apparent need for training in preservation skills for the craftsmen who are to do the work within the libraries of the country. Here, the problem is in part, a sociological one due to the gap between the "Professional" levels and the workmen, the craftsmen who must do the repairing and the binding of books and manuscripts. Where the librarians of the collections I have seen, have been broken in the best sense of the word he has been a scholar there has very evident condescension towards the craftsmen quite inconsistent with the genuine humility which is the mark of the true scholar."

This is the second major handicap that is being faced by the librarians. Unless books, manuscripts and records are carefully preserved against the vagaries of nature for the use of the posterity, there is no use in being complacently satisfied about the possession of a rich collection of books. Preservation of records up to a maximum extent should be the criterion of the managements and personnel concerned in libraries. In India, the librarians are incharge of books and the curators of manuscripts for their proper upkeep and preservation. As such, it is the duty of those technical people—librarians and curators to find ways and means for proper preservation of the materials collected and stored. This needs thorough practical knowledge.

The main deteriorative agents of record materials are :

(a) **Atmospheric Pollution** : The sulphur diodide present in the polluted air in industrial towns is one of the principal causes for the deterioration of paper.

(b) **Effects of Light** : The discolouration and eventual embrittlement of newsprint or similar paper made of mechanical woodpulp when exposed to the action of sunlight is a well known phenomenon. Paper of good quality is also susceptible to deterioration by direct exposure of light though the deterioration may occur without discolouration. Direct sun-light should be regarded as a potential destroyer of all forms of record materials such as paper, parchment, leather etc.

(c) **Effects of Dust** : Dust consists largely of small angular particles of silicous material. These particles are so small that they become embedded between the fibres of the leather, cloth and paper.

(d) **Variation in Temperature and Humidity** : Paper parchment cloth, thread, adhesives and leather, the organic constituents of records are susceptible to decay from chemical changes brought about by exterior influences such as sulphur dioxide in the air.

(e) **Mildew** : This is a variety of vegetable organism which propagates by means of spores, which are always present in the air. They can remain dormant for an indefinite period until conditions become ripe for their growth. The incidence of mildew is found most in volumes and books which remain pressed against each other.

(f) **Insects** (book worms, silver lices and cockroaches) : No repository is completely free from insects and the protection of records from the depredation of insects in one of the most serious and difficult problems of the archivist, climatic conditions render this problem more acute in the topics. The cellulose in paper and fabrics attracts certain kinds of insects. Some kinds of insects are also particularly found in other records materials such as glue, starch and casing.

(g) Careless use and handling is the person's direct contact which deteriorates the life of the records. One must have the sense of duty to handle it carefully.

The above mentioned deteriorative agents of records can be remedied in the following manner :

A. **Storage** : The design of storage rooms and bookstacks should facilitate this by reducing the number of possible lodging places and allowing those that must remain to be cleaned with case. Good ventilation and elimination of excessive heat or damp also assist in this. Most of the pests dislike sun-light but unfortunately sunlight is also harmful to paper. It is hardly necessary to say that only fire and insect-proof materials should be used for the construction of the stacks.

B. **Air-conditioning** : This solves many of the problems of record preservation and the money spent on air-conditioning ultimately proves economical as it saves a good deal of repairing and binding expenses.

C. **Insecticides** : The most common and widely used insecticide is Naphthalene which under normal conditions is more of a deterrent than killer. Other insecticides like Neocid, D.D.T. and Renu preservation oils are also used. Thymol fumigation, Paradichlorobenzene fumigation and Vacuum fumigation are also the other type of functions that act as insecticides.

Practical methods of cleaning and repair of records are feathering of folded records, washing and removal of stains, reinforcing the torn or brittle paper and binding of volumes and application of leather preservative dressing.

Microfilming and Photographic Services and Processing

Modern libreries have not been behind in taking advantage of the great developments in photographic reproduction, not only for obtaining texts which would otherwise be unobtainable but also for supplying outside readers with copies or extracts. Their use and potentialities, accommodation and safety conditions have for some years engaged the attention of libraries and commercial organisations. Such facilities, no doubt however, involve extra expenses and are still too small to provide with promptitude all that is needed. Fuller provision of apparatus for reading is also required and the damand is bound to increase. The need for a central record of the large body of reproductions which will accumulate is increasingly felt and it is important that measures be taken without delay to provide a union catalogue.

The use of microfilm is an advantage for the preservation of back periodical files. Use of microfilm results in great saving of shelf space. The conventional bound volumes need 7½ times more space to house them than do microfilm reels for the same number of volumes. If the microfilms are regularly supplied by the commerical firms, the problem of ones own missing or mutilated issues is solved. The cost of binding as against the cost of microfilm is much more in the long run. The initial cost of a microfilm programme is expensive because much initial investment is needed to purchase of equipment, readers and humidified storage cabinets. The advantages of microfilming are many and the most important are that rate and out of print books can be reproduced and missing isues of journals that are not available can also be microfilmed and preserved. Secondly, there is the saving of shelf-space in a growing library. Microcards and Microcards-in-punched cards are also in vogue which also supplement microfilms. Microfilming needs proper projectors to film the materials so required and the microfilm require operating projectors screen them for reading purposes, whereas microcards need micro-card readers. The disadvantages are few. They need only skilled operation of the apparatus and equipment and secondly the coloured illustrations are produced in black and white rather than the original. This disadvantage can be surmounted if proper practical training in the field is given.

In Western countries, the preservation of the conventional type of bound volumes is slowly being replaced by the modern method of microfilming preservation. Modern libraries which spend a good part of their budgets on back volumes of journals can as well go in for purchasing a Microfilming plant and other necessary processing accessories and can have a microfilm reproduction of the volumes and thus save the amount in spending on a number of library stacks etc., and also to save extra expenses incurred in preservation and care of those old types of books. Microfilmed article if projected on a screen, can be referred to at a time by a number of research fellows and thus save the time in the circulation process and reservation processes of books.

Remedial Measures : A suggestion

The impact of the various technical handicaps referred to above is felt more in the University Libraries. After Independence, the universities are being financed and developed by the University Grants Commission. The U.G.C. is having a number of committees to advise and develop on all branches of university education i.e., development of post-graduate studies in science and humanities ; technology and research. Research in any branch of study of technical and scientific development needs a proper library. There is a library sub-committee of the U.G.C., which finances and advises the U.G.C. in matter connected with the construction of suitable buildings, provision of equipment, the purchase of books by way of Recurring and Non-recurring grants, etc. While thanking the U.G.C. for its generous attitude in giving large grants for the improvement of the library in extending its reference service they can also be approached for financial assistance to avoid the technical handicaps faced by the University libraries.

The U.G.C. can make a separate provision for the improvement of the techical sections like, bindery with equipment (press, cutting machine etc.,) ; a small laboratory for preparing preservation oils and to equip with necessary clearing and cleaning materials (vacuum cleaners, fumigation chambers etc.,) and lastly a dark room for photography, microfilming and processing and its equipment like microfilming camera, projector with screen and processing materials. Substantial grants towards recurring and non-recurring expenditure should be given for the smooth running of the different sections. Although the need is felt, no single university can afford to incur this extra expenditure to train the staff in those particular fields.

To remedy the technical handicaps in practical training a refresher course of six eight weeks duration should be organised. It is suggested that the university library, Delhi would be a suitable institution where this course can be conducted. Other institutions which may organise such courses may be the INSDOC, Delhi specialised in Microfilming reproduction ; Bhandarkar Oriental Research Institue, Pune.—specialised in preservation of records, manuscripts and books etc. If the U.G.C. is apprised of the necessity and convinced of the situation, it can undoubtedly shoulder the responsibility to run such refresher courses. Wherever, the training is conducted the total period should not exceed more than six to eight weeks. The training can be had once in a year, preferably between April and June when the University colleges are closed for the vacation. If the U.G.C. agrees to finance the entire expenditure incurred for the refresher course, the universities will definitely depute their professional men, to undergo the course.

There is no doubt that the University Grants Commission will accept the suggestion if the matter is put forth before them by proper persons like, Shri B.S. Kesavan, Director, INSDOC, New Delhi, and other prominent librarians. There would not be any difficulty since the U.G.C. has already taken part in many projects to help improve the development of libraries, especially the university libraries to enrich reference services and to synchronise with the modern trends of the scientific and technological age.

The U.G.C. in collaboration with the India Wheat Loan Educational Exchange programme has deputed a number of librarians to the U.S.A. on study tours to study various problems in connection with the development of university libraries and to run the libraries in India on the same lines. Secondly, the U.G.C. has sponsored many workshops at various centres in India to exchange the views in regard to the much discussed problems in the development of the University Libraries. As such, it is hoped if proper approach is made, to the U.G.C. in this regard also, the U.G.C. will unsparingly extend its cooperation in remedying the technical handicaps of the librarian in India and thus help in fostering the development of university libraries.

The successful professional worker must continue to learn during the entire course of the professional life. Success in a profession depends not only on the skill acquired but on the insight, judgement and ability to meet the changing situations.

REFERENCES

Cockrell, Douglass—Book Binding & the Care of Books.

"Research in the Humanity and the Social Science"—Report of a survey by the British Academy—1961.

College & Research Libraries—Vol. 21—May 1960.

Summary of the Recommendations made by Mr. John Alden, U.S. Librarian regarding Books Preservation and Book Binding—Presented to The Librarian, of National Library, Calcutta.

SPECIALIST LIBRARIES
A Survey in Andhra Pradesh

This survey of special libraries in Andhra Pradesh projects an image which is not so optimistic. It is also evident from the information gathered that most of the special libraries are being organized, administered merely at the house-keeping level. A great deal of effort, money and manpower have to be put in so that they gear their services to the research level. The overall picture of special library services not being highly encouraging, it is suggested that the State Government should explore the possibilities of improving the services by providing necessary facilities in all aspects.

Special libraries, particularly technical libraries, do not have as old a history as libraianship itself. Special libraries serve a particular group of community interested in a particular field. The activities of a special library should, therefore, be diverted to a common purpose and defined goal, taking into account the research and other needs of the clientele they serve.

From the available sources, it is estimated that there are about two hundred special libraries in the State of Andhra Pradesh. Of these again, the number of Specialist Libraries as termed by S.R. Ranganathan would be about eighty.

However, for purposes of the present survey, the following types of libraries have been covered :

I. Professional-cum-Academic Institutions

1. Oriental Colleges and Institutes
2. Engineering
3. Technical Education Institutes

4. Agriculture
5. Veterinary
6. Medical
7. Music
8. Teacher's Training
9. Physical Education
10. Law

II. Government and Research Departments

1. Departmental and Legislature Libraries
2. Research Stations
3. Learned Societies

III. Industries

1. Business
2. Commercial Firms
3. Insurance and Banks

Libraries, in general, play a vital role in disseminating latest information to its users. It is incumbent on special libraries to discharge this function more expeditiously to avoid any possible duplication of research being undertaken within the parent organization.

A questionnaire was prepared and sent to special libraries in Andhra Pradesh. The following reference tools were consulted in locating the special libraries located in Andhra Pradesh.

1. Andhra Pradesh Almanac, 1968 ;
2. Research Facilities in Hyderabad ;
3. IASLIC : Directory of Special Libraries in India ;
4. Times of India Directory and Year Book, including Who is Who, 1971 ;
5. Handbook of Universities in India and Ceylon, 1971 ; and
6. Directory of Scientific Research Institutions in India, 1969

After consulting the above mentioned reference tools, a total of 178 libraries attached to various organizations as also Government Departments were selected as special libraries for the purpose of this survey. The questionnaire referred to above was sent in duplicate to all these 178 libraries with a request to return the same duly filled in, within a stipulated time. As not many replies were received within the prescribed time-limit, the institutions were reminded to expedite replies. In spite of this, the response was very poor. Personal visits were paid to as many libraries as possible in Hyderabad where more than 60 per cent of the libraries which were addressed, are situated.

Out of 178 organizations, only 46 responded. This works out to only 26 per cent of the total replies whlch should have been received. Out of the 46 replies, only 32 have furnished the relevant information in the questionnaire, of the remaining 14, four replied saying that no libraries worth the name are attached to them. Insufficient information was received from six libraries. Two libraries sent interim replies saying that full information would be sent later on but this was never received. Two sent some ready-made literature about their libraries, which could not answer all the points in the questionnaire.

The 32 libraries that submitted relevant information are distributed throughout the State as follows :

Hyderabad city	14
Tirupati	6
Visakhapatnam	1
Rajahmundry	2
Guntur Dist.	2
Cuddapah Dist.	2
Nellore Dist.	2
Warangal	1
Kakinada	1
Rudrur (Nizamabad Dist.)	1

The libraries surveyed are grouped into three broad categories, viz.,

(i) Industrial Libraries

(ii) Research Libraries including those serving the judiciary and the legislature and other departments of Government and

(iii) Academic-cum-research Libraries.

Industrial Libraries

Besides a few chemicals, oil, tannery and paper industries, Andhra Pradesh has the following industries (Number of industries is given in the bracket) :

Cashewnut (32) ; Cement (11) ; Fertilizer (28) ; Metal (50) ; Mica (42) ; Mining (5) ; Sugar (38) ; Textile (18) ; Tobacco (300) ; and Engineering (180).

Small industries are also predominant. To help improve the quality of industries, a Small Industry Extension Training Institute (SIET) was established in Hyderabad by the Government of India in 1962.

According to the survey, it is observed that there are only five industrial libraries in the State worth-mentioning. These libraries are well-equipped, scientifically organized and help its clientele with documentation services. The subject-wise distribution of these five libraries is given in Table 1.

TABLE 1

Subject-wise Break-up of Libraries

	Industries	Libraries
Industry (General)	3	1
Electronics	2	1
Machine tools	2	1
Aeronautics	1	1
Shipping	2	1
Total	10	5

The entire research activities is centred round the city of Hyderabad, the capital of Andhra Pradesh. Most of the research libraries are established at Hyderabad during the Second Plan period.

Out of these 97 research institutions, replies were received only from 15 libraries, and these only have been covered in this survey.

There are four universities and 235 colleges in the State. The university libraries except the Andhra Pradesh Agricultural University and the libraries of arts sciences and commerce colleges are excluded from this survey. Only professional colleges are included.

TABLE 2

Research Institutions and Libraries

CC	Subject	Number of Institutions	Number of Libraries
Z4	Orientalia	5	1
C	Physics	5	2
D	Engineering	5	1
F	Technology	2	—
G	Biology	2	—
H	Geology	2	1
J	Agriculturae	25	4
L	Medicine	6	1
LX	Pharmacology	1	—
MZZ	Humanities	6	2
NZ	Languages & Literature	3	—
SZ	Social Science	12	1
T	Education	5	2
X	Economics	4	—
X5	Commerce	8	—
W	Political Science	3	—
Y7	Anthropology	2	—
Z	Law	1	—
	Total	97	15

TABLE 3

Academic Institutions and Libraries

CC	Subject	Number of Institutions	Number of Libraries
Z4	Oriental Colleges	8	1
D	Engineering	6	1
	Polytechnics	21	3
J	Agriculture	3	3
KX	Veterinary	3	—
L	Medicine	10	4
NR	Music	2	—
T	Education	16	1
Z	Law	2	—
	Total	71	13

Out of the 71 academic-cum-teaching institutions, data were received only from 12. Sri Venkateswara Oriental College, managed by the Tirumala-Tirupati Devasthanams, Tirupati, established in 1884 is the oldest college in the State.

There are four Institutions in Tirupati serving the cause of Oriental Learning by providing study and research in ancient Sastras and Hindu Culture (Sanathana Dharma) through the medium of Sanskrit or English. They are (1) Sri Venkateswara Oriental College (1884) ; (2) Sri Venkateswara University Oriental Research Institute (1940) ; (3) Sri Venkateswara University College (1954) ; (4) Kendriya Sanskrit Vidyapeetha (1962).

Data on the Basis of Questionnaire

A. Preliminaries :

Table 4 shows the break-up of libraries established yearwise and the total number :

TABLE 4

Year-wise Establishment of Libraries

Period	No. of Institutions Established During the Period
1881—1890	1
1891—1900	1
1901--1910	—
1911—1920	2
1921—1930	1
1931—1940	3
1941—1950	4
1951—1960	12
1961—1970	8
Total	32

A number of institutions were established during the Second Five Year Plan period.

Table 5 gives a picture about the number of users in the special libraries covered :

TABLE 5

Library Users During a Year

No. of Users During a Year	No. of Libraries
Below 100	8
101— 250	4
251— 500	8
501— 750	4
751—1000	3
1001—1250*	—
1251—1500	3
1501—1750*	—
1751—2000*	1

In the above table the unit of 250 readers is taken to represent the range of numbers. So, no information is furnished against these figures as the data given by the libraries do not fall within these particular ranges.

Out of the 32 libraries of various types, only three libraries (Agricultural College, Bapatla ; Medical College, Guntur ; and Regional Research Laboratory, Hyderabad) are housed in separate buildings, 4 in separate halls, in their parent office buildings and 23 libraries are housed in some portion in the main building. This evidently reveals that a majority of the libraries surveyed do not have independent buildings.

The Table 6 gives an idea of the size of the book collection in the 32 libraries, which, together, have a book stock of 3, 73, 750.

The book collection includes back volumes of journals, pamphlets, manuscripts, standards and specifications and other non-book materials.

Out of 32 libraries, three libraries have not furnished this information. This value entirely depends upon the number of books, nature of collection, and types of libraries. This value includes all the documents, both books and non-book material. The total value estimated is Rs. 74,19,144. The largest collection of books is in American Studies Research Centre, Hyderabad (53085) and the smallest is in Millet Research Station, Podalakur (29).

Table 7 gives the break-up of libraries on the basis of the number of journals subscribed to. About 4,100 periodicals are currently received in all the libraries taken together. But many of these might be multiple copies. In all, there might be about 3,000 different individual scientific periodicals in the libraries covered.

TABLE 6

Book Collection in Libraries*

Size of book collection	Number of Libraries
Below 1000	6
1001 — 5000	2
5001 —10,000	9
10,001—15,000	10
15,001—20,000*	—
20,001—25,000	1
25,001—30,000	1
30,001—35,000*	—
35,001—40,000	2
40,001 and above	1

* In the above table, the unit of 5000 books is taken to represent the range of books. So, no information is furnished against these figures as the data given by the libraries do not fall within these particular ranges.

TABLE 7

Number of Journals Subscribed by Libraries

No. of periodicals subscribed to	Number of Libraries
Below 50	11
51—100	5
101—150	4
151—200	4
201—250	3
251—300*	—
301—350	1
351—400	2
401—450	—
451 and above	1

* The unit of 50 periodicals is taken to represent the range of periodicals subscribed to. So, no information is furnished against these figures as the data given by the libraries do not fall within these particular ranges.

The total amount spent on subscription to journals varies from library to library, depending on the number and types of journals and resources of the library. The total amount spent on subscription to journals by all the libraries put together is Rs. 4,56,140.

The distribution of documents other than books and journals in all the libraries taken together is as follows :

Standards and specifications	6,000
Manuscripts	3,000
Palmleaf Manuscripts	14,000
Trade catalogues	10,000

Out of 32 libraries surveyed, only 24 have professionally qualified staff. The remaining libraries are managed by clerical and non-professional staff. The staff for documentation work are employed in a few industrial libraries. The persons incharge of the libraries are designated as Librarians, Documentalists, Technical Assistants and Technical Information Officers, and Library Officers, etc.

Out of the 32 libraries surveyed, only 12 have Committees. In the remaining libraries Library Committees do not exist.

Almost all the libraries have furnished Information regarding expenditure on books and periodicals only. In the absence of information regarding expenditure on staff, furniture, fittings, etc., in the library budget, the percentage in relation to the total budget of the organization could not be worked out.

Fifteen libraries follow the Dewey Decimal Classification. The distribution in the 32 libraries according to the scheme of classification used is given below :

Decimal classification	:	15
U.D.C.	:	8
C.C.	:	1
No Scientific Scheme	:	8
Total	:	32

As for the type and form of catalogue, the 32 libraries can be analysed as under :

Type of Catalogue		**No. of Libraries**
Dictionary	:	11
Classified	:	12
Dictionary & Classified	:	2
No Type	:	7
Form of Catalogue used		
Card	:	19
Ledger	:	6
Card & Ledger	:	2
No Form	:	5
Presentation of Catalogue		
Typed	:	15
Handwritten	:	7
Typed & Handwritten	:	1
Specific Information not Supplied	:	9
Shelf list		
Libraries having shelf list	:	16
Libraries not having shelf list	:	16
Accessioning		
Card	:	2
Register	:	25
Sheets	:	1
None	:	4

Out of the 32 libraries, only 25 libraries have furnished this information. The total number of books issued, consulted, etc., per day for all libraries, put together on an average, is an under :

Issue per day	..	51
Consultation per day on an average	..	98
Attendance per day on an average	..	66

Out of 32 libraries surveyed, almost all the libraries work during the working hours of the parent organization. These timings vary from 9.00 a.m. to 5.00 p.m., 10.35 a.m. to 5.30 p.m. ; or twice a day from 8.00 a.m. to 11.00 a.m. and from 2.00 p.m. to 5.00 p.m. Unlike public and academic libraries which are open to readers for about 12 hours a day, these libraries are open for only 6 to 8 hours a day.

Only ten libraries have adopted some recognized method of issue like Browne, Newark and Dickman. A few libraries maintain an issue register of the conventional type for issue of books. A few libraries have replied that they follow "their own method" for issue of books.

Twenty libraries follow open access. Two libraries provide free access only to their staff members and not to others. The remaining follow closed access.

In all the libraries surveyed, stock verification is a routine, done every year. As for the method followed, four libraries use shelf list. Others follow the procedure of checking the books with the help of Accession Registers of Stock Registers.

Only ten libraries do not hold the librarian responsible for loss of books and the rest hold him responsible, excepting two libraries which have not taken any decision in the matter. The remaining libraries, however, hold the library staff responsible for loss of books.

Only ten libraries provide Reference and Documentation Service. Even out of these ten libraries, six libraries undertake reference service of a general type, i.e., person-to-person-contact, in answering queries, in bringing out the list of recent additions, in preparation of bibliographies, etc. The remaining 16 libraries provide systematic documentation service to the users of those libraries. The types of services provided are :

(a) Issuing a periodical list of additions and current awareness list ;
(b) Compilation of bibliographies in anticipation and on demand ;
(c) Press-clipping service ;
(d) Routing of periodicals according to subject interest of the individual departments ;
(e) Answering reference queries by oral as well as written communication ;

(f) Indexing and abstracting ;
(g) Commercial and technical information services ;
(h) Bibliographical and newsbrief Service ;
(i) On-the-spot reference service ;
(j) Translation service being undertaken with the help of INSDOC and IASLIC ;
(k) Current content reprint service.

Reference service of general type is being rendered by the libraries attached to learned societies, professional educational institutions, etc. However, documentation service is being provided by the libraries attached to industrial and commercial institutions.

Many of the libraries serving industries and research institutions do not have their own translation facility. These and other libraries procure translations through various sources, such as the INSDOC and IASLIC.

Seven libraries, viz., the Institution of Asian Studies, National Geophysical Research Institute, National Institute of Nutrition, Regional Research Laboratory, Hindusthan Aeronautics, Hindusthan Machine Tools and SIET have their own reprography service which is provided to their clientele.

Out of 32 libraries, only eight libraries have their own Binding Section with necessary equipment and their own staff. Sixteen Libraries get their work executed through commercial binders. The remaining eight libraries have not furnished any information on this point.

Findings

The following are some of the distinctive features of these special libraries :

(a) They are attached to industrial organizations, professional institutions and learned societies, forming part of their parent organizations ;
(b) They have specific rather than general objectives and are specialized in particular subject fields and their closely related areas ;
(c) Their clientele are specialists in some subject fields and serve their parent organizations with special interest ;
(d) They have mainly been established to meet the vital need for research and to provide their clientele with expeditious documentation and reprographic service ;

(e) A majority of them have small, specialized collections and small staff ;

(f) For them the latest information on their subject fields is more important, and this, they process for being disseminated quickly to their clientele ;

(g) Many of the libraries possess technical reports, standards and specifications, patents, reprints of research papers, trade literature, etc., and two of them have paper and palm leaf manuscripts.

Similarities

(a) Their primary aim is research and in that pursuit, all of them are concerned to serve their clientele to the maximum extent ;

(b) All these libraries possess in their stock, material needed by their clientele in the form of books and non-book material. The difference is found only in the approach of technical services like classification, indexing and reference service.

Differences

(a) Industrial and Research Libraries follow depth classification, use classified catalogue and provide documentation service, whereas the academic-cum-research libraries follow broad classification, use dictionary catalogue and provide general reference service.

(b) The first two types of libraries have adopted modern technique of library service and are providing the research and industrial organizations with the latest information and nascent thought pinpointedly, exhaustively and expeditiously to help improve the scientific, technological and industrial progress of the state in particular and the nation in general. The remaining libraries are concerned mainly with providing to their clientele with the usual library facilities and information on the research undertaken.

The difference between libraries of the various library organization types-Societies (Learned and Professional) ; Government (Administrative and Research Depts.) ; and Business, (Industrial, Industrial research and commercial) is that the business organization proves better than the other two for the simple reason that private enterprises with their ingenuity, skills and reseources, compete with the public enterprises and prove themselves better not only in earning profits with their quality products but also in attracting highly qualified scientists and research workers to exhibit their talent and efficiency in the field of scientific research, which is considered the backbone for the prosperity of the country as a whole. In Government organizations their research departments are geard up for two main purposes, viz.,

(a) research for defence services—army, navy and airforce,

(b) research for the benefit of industry, agriculture and medicine ; and

(c) research in social sciences and humanities is found to be far less when compared to the research in science and technology.

It is also observed that effective steps have not been taken by any of the parent organizations of the libraries with regard to inter-library co-operation, which alone could save the precious time of the libraries and their users. Co-operation among libraries may be extended in the sphere of acquisition, storage and inter-library loan.

Recommendations

The special library is a major source of information in the organization it serves. The special library acquires, organizes, maintains, utilises and disseminates informational materials germane to the organization's activities.

The librarian in the special library shall be responsible for all administrative and professional functions of the library. He should be a professional librarian who can, by virtue of his education, subject speciality, experience and personal qualifications successfully carries out the objectives and functions of the special library. It is important that professional members of the special library staff participate in professional societies, seminars, etc. concerned with their specialities. Specialists other than librarians may be part of the library staff. The professional staff of the library should be creative, inventive, ingenious and productive from the view point of management's expectations.

However, the survey has revealed that not all libraries have professionally qualified staff. Four of the libraries are managed by members of the staff of the parent organization. Two institutions have replied that they do not find the need to have professionally qualified library staff on the plea that their collection is small.

We would like to suggest that it is absolutely necessary to have professionally qualified librarians in special libraries irrespective of the size of the collection. This is suggested in the interest of the efficient working of the parent organization. The size of the library holdings will be growing year by year in keeping with the widening scope of the parent organization, and in view of this, the appointment of a qualified librarian will be a valuable asset to the management. It is appropriate to quote here what J. Loeb has stated as far back as 1932, regarding the importance of the library, "Real discoveries are actually made in the library and subsequently tested out in the laboratory."

Out of 32 libraries only 12 have Committees. For the proper functioning of the library it is necessary to have a Committee to guide and assist the librarian in the discharge of his duties. The Committee should be responsible for laying down the policies of the library. The librarian should function as the member-secretary of the Committee.

Collection and Services

1. **Collection** : The subject coverage of the library's collection should be intensive and exhaustive enough to meet the current and anticipated information requirements of the library's clientele. The special library's collection should be fairly representative in relation to the organization's special needs. Acquisition policies of a special library must be established within the framework of the library's stated objectives. The special library staff should be responsible for the efficient organization of materials and for making available tools like the catalogues, indexes, bulletins, bibliographies and documentation lists for locating the required materials and the information promptly.

2. **Services** : In addition to supplying comprehensive and current information required by scientists and research workers, the special library staff will involve themselves in compilation of bibliographies on special topics, issuing of library bulletins, translation service, maintaining files of research reports and trade literature, relative indexes and other personalized services of various types. Publications not in stock in the library or in the organization should be obtained from other libraries or institutions, on inter-library loan. There should also be a policy for co-operative acquisition, storage

and retrieval to save money and time on individual organizations. An effective system for maximum utilization of current periodical literature should be an integral part of the special library's service programme.

Stock

The libraries surveyed have varying stocks of books and journals the smallest collection representing a stock of 29 books and 4 journals and the largest one representing 53085 books and 516 journals. One of the libraries has in stock 17000 manuscripts comprising palm leaf and paper manuscripts.

The crux of providing an efficient information service in libraries in general and special libraries in particular, lies in the number of periodicals being received in the libraries and their proper processing. Comprehensive compilation of bibliographies, documentation lists, current awareness lists, etc., will be directly dependent in proportion to the number of journals being received. This being so, it is incumbent on the authorities of the special libraries to acquire the maximum number of required periodicals and to provide adequate money for the same in the annual budgets.

Processing

As for the scheme adopted for classifying the reading materials, only one library has adopted the CC. Of the remaining, 15 have adopted the DC, 8 UDC and 1 does not follow any scientific scheme. It would be advisable if more libraries adopt the CC because of its uniqueness in fact analysis, which alone helps in speedier retrieval and dissemination of information.

It may be noted here, that library co-operation restricted to inter-library loan only exists among the libraries. Other equally important activities like co-operative acquisition, co-operative cataloguing, co-operative storage and retrieval are not practised and carried on. It is suggested that the authorities of special libraries should recognise the importance of co-operative activities among libraries and take necessary steps for effective implementation, resulting in saving of time and money.

The special library should be centrally located for the benefit of its users. Long-term planning on the location of the special library as a separate building is important. Necessary provision should be made for the safety and security of the library materials and creation of effective working conditions for staff and users. Serious thought should be given for space and adequate reading and office space and necessary equipments.

Of the libraries surveyed, only three are housed in independent buildings. Others are housed in halls forming part of the main building. One library is housed in a small room of 10'x10'. The library is generally described as "the heart of an institution", "A laboratory and a workshop for the scholar", etc. The spirit of these quotations should be realized and fostered by the authorities by providing a well-planned and centrally located building in the parent organization.

The budget of a special library should be prepared on the recommendations of the librarian. About 15% of the total budget allotted for the organization should be provided exclusively for the library for rendering efficient service. It is also recommended that out of this outlay a greater proportion be allocated for staff. Out of the allotment made for books and periodicals, more amount should be spent on 'Periodical literature'. As far as possible, the librarian should have the power to incur the expenditure from out of the budgeted funds.

Having realized the magnitude of the problem of information explosion, the professional librarian has to supply the urgently needed information to the users and the researcher. These, in turn, have to 'keep up' with the current information, and will also be concerned as to how best to have bibliographic control over the information material currently produced for being disseminated for fruitful utilization. "Organization of documentation and information services have now become the essential prerequisites of modern librarianship, in keeping with the predominated trend of contemporary culture of specialization. This is true of the special library in particular".

Further Suggestions

(a) The National Science Library at Delhi should promote and co-ordinate the activities of special libraries in India.

(b) It may also establish its branches in different regions for this purpose.

(c) It should also function as a clearing-house for scientific information.

(d) In addition, it should establish liaison with international scientific libraries and information centres.

(e) Finally, it should provide expert advice in the planning of special library services in the country.

This survey of special libraries in Andhra Pradesh projects an image which is not very optimistic. Most of the libraries need to be provided with adequate finance and better staff as also centrally located buildings. It is only by satisfying these conditions that it is possible to provide efficient and effective library service. It is, however, evident from the information received that most of the special libraries are being organized and administered merely at the housekeeping level. A great deal of effort, money and manpower have to be put in, so that they could gear their services to the research level. Andhra Pradesh is rich in agricultural and industrial potential in addition to the concentration of centrally-administered, private and public undertakings in Hyderabad. Next to Hyderabad, Viskhapatnam has the industrial complex like ship building, oil refinery, steel and heavy plates and vessels. Along with these major industries, many subsidiary industries have also sprung up. In addition, there are a number of institutions providing professional education. All these industries as well as educational institutions need to be provided with efficient library service. As remarked elsewhere in this survey, the overall picture of special library services not being highly encouraging, we suggest that the State Government should explore the possibilities of improving the services for the prosperity of Andhra Pradesh in particular and the country in general.

REFERENCES

Subbarayan, Ed. : Andhra Pradesh Almanac—1968. Madras, The Educational Products of India, 1967.

Loeb, J : Library's place in research. Ex. libris 1 Sept. 1923, p. 74, quoted in Strauss & Others : Scientific and technical libraries : Their organization and administration N.Y. Wiley, 1964, p. 18.

Mukherjee, A. K. : Fundamental of Special Librarianship and Documentation (IASLIC Manual No. 1), Calcutta, IASLIC, 1969.

COLLEGE LIBRARIES IN ANDHRA PRADESH I

S.V. University College Libraries

Library is now recognised as an important social institution in the life of any community, where every person can seek every kind of knowledge. With the development in the art of production of recorded knowledge, libraries have expanded in size and enlarged their services. An academic library is, therefore, an important educational tool in a College. No Science College can function without laboratories. A laboratory in a College serves only a branch of knowledge but a library contains material in all branches of knowledge.

The Importance of a library in a college has been stressed by every University Education Commission. I will content myself by quoting one or two. (1) Report of Dr. S.R. Ranganathan, 1948 : "Training in higher branches of learning and research is mainly a question of learning how to use the tools and if the library tools are not there, how can the student learn to use them ?" (2) President Truman's Commission on Higher Education say, "The library is second only to the instructional staff in its importance for high quality of instruction and research". Therefore, the present day College should have a well-planned and functional library, so that the graduate leaving the institution may be able to meet the increasing demands of the individual intelligence and intellectual capabilities in the changing social, political and economic conditions in our country.

Let me quote here the impression of the college library formed by one of the reputed Government College principals of our University area.

"As a teacher in a college, my experience has been that most of the colleges which have come up recently have no building worth the name or where they have, they have very inadequate accommodation for the ever-growing student population. A college library is still considered as desirable and it is treated as supplementary or rather subsidiary adjunct to the college. In some colleges, libraries as such, do not exist. Even where they do exist, they are far below the average standard, far behind the times and designed in terms of functions quite different from the services expected of them, and exist merely as decorative adjuncts, probably, to fulfil one of the conditions of affiliation to the University".

Let me say what exactly are the causes for this unhappy situation ? The following are the few, for which proper solutions have to be found out and implemented.

1. The management and the administration have not so far realised that a library is an integral part of a college, since there is a confusion of purpose. No conscious effort is made for book provision and its administration.
2. Meagre financial resources.
3. Inadequate library accommodation.
4. Ignoring appointment of qualified and competent Librarian and supporting staff.
5. Curriculum and method of instruction.
6. Non-interested faculty members.
7. Lack of love of reading in student community.

This sad situation, which was observed by me when I personally visited one of the oldest and richest of the College Libraries in the University area, prompted me to take up this project of "Surveying the existing conditions of College Libraries in Andhra Pradesh" and to suggest certain standards and norms for their efficient functioning.

Evaluation of the Existing Conditions of College Libraries in Andhra Pradesh

Objectives

(a) To know the existing conditions of libraries and to see how far the minimum standards are maintained.

(b) To identify the differences in existing conditions of College Libraries under different managements.

(c) To identify the differences in the existing conditions of the College Libraries in the semi-urban and urban areas.

(d) To suggest measures for improving the existing conditions of libraries.

Scope

The present study attempts to reveal the existing conditions of College Libraries in Andhra Pradesh. The emphasis is on 'Fact-finding'. College Libraries for this purpose include only Arts, Science and Commerce Colleges. For the sake of convenience, clarity, and uniformity, the following categories of Colleges are excluded—Medical, Engineering and Polytechnic (Nehru Technological University, A.P.), (Agricultural University, A,P.) ; and Oriental Colleges. The area is confined to the colleges affiliated to Sri Venkateswara, Andhra and Osmania Universities situated in Andhra Pradesh.

Origin of Andhra Pradesh

The self-immolation of Sri Potti Sri Ramulu paved the way for the separate state of Andhra in 1952. This was followed by the formation of the present Andhra Pradesh in 1953 comprising the former Andhra State and the Telengana region. The State comprises of 22 districts.

Literacy Percentage*

Urban or Rural	Men	Women	Total
Urban	57.30 (61.28)	36.31 (42.26)	47.08 (52.49)
Rural	27.31 (33.76)	10.92 (13.17)	19.19 (23.74)
Total	33.18 (39.45)	5.75 (18.72)	24.57 (29.46)

Note :—Figures within brackets under each entry indicate the corresponding all India percentage.

* *Source* : Pocket book of population on Statistics Registrar—General and Census Commissioner, New Delhi, 1972.

Historical Background of College Libraries in Andhra Pradesh

College Libraries themselves cannot be independent and isolated institutions but have to be ancillary in nature. They are appended to educational institutions and reflect their aims and objectives through the Library services. As such, the history of educational institutions (colleges) forms the background for the history of college libraries also. The origin and growth of college libraries have to be traced and trekked along with the educational institutions to which they are attached. Historically, the development of education in Andhra Pradesh can be brodly divided into the following stages : Pre-Buddhistic ; Buddhistic ; Hindu Ages between 16-19 centuries ; British ; and Post-Independence. Higher education and its impact on Andhra Pradesh state is also disscussed. Contributing factors for progressive educational policies, establishment of higher educational institutions are also touched upon.

Educational System

As regards higher education, the state of Andhra Pradesh has three universities viz. Osmania University, established in 1918, with jurisdiction over the Telengana region, the Andhra University, established in 1926, with jurisdiction over coastal Andhra districts of Srikakulam, Visakhapatnam, East Godavari, West Godavari, Krishna, Prakasam and Guntur, and the Sri Venkateswara University, established in 1954, with jurisdiction over the districts of Nellore, Chittoor, Cuddapah, Anantapur and Kurnool. Increase in the number of colleges year after year and also the increasing demand for post-graduates in various sectors of development warranted the establishment of three post-graduate centres in the State during 1967-73. The three centres are Warangal in Osmania University area, Guntur in Andhra University area, and Anantapur in Sri Venkateswara University area.

Each university in the state is both a teaching and an affiliating university. The affiliated colleges, which are managed by the government and private bodies, provide for under-graduate courses. There are separate colleges for women, and most of the colleges for men are co-educational in character. Evening colleges have also been established for the benefit of employees.

The Educational system gives an overall picture of the system of education in Andhra Pradesh. The nationally recommended 10+2+3 structure has already been introduced in the state. Generally, a child joins the regular stream of schooling at the age of 5 splus. Provision is also available to some extent for pre-primary education of children belonging to the age group 3-4. The primary stage extends to 5 years. This is followed by a two-year course of upper primary or middle education. Thus, the child in the normal course joins a secondary school at the age of 11 plus and takes a three year course there. The pupil takes a public examination at the course, by which time he would have reached the age of 15 plus. The intermediate or higher secondary course offered in the junior colleges for secondary school leavers is of two years duration. Students who take to professional course like primary teachers training, polytechnic education, engineering, medical education etc. divert from the main track of general education just before or after the intermediate course. The first degree course is of three years duration followed by a two years course for M.A., M.Sc., M.Com, or M.B.A.

Besides the above said three Universities during 1977-78, three more P.G. courses centres were established at Cuddapah, Kurnool and Kavali with specialization in Economics, Statistics and Commerce and Political Science.

TABLE 2

Educational Institutions in 1973-74

Category of Institution	Number	Enrolment Boys	Girls	Total	No. of Teachers
Pre-Primary	67	9,527	7,533	17,060	117
Primary/Jr. Basic	36,772	24,21,518	15,90,646	40,12,614	79,067
Middle/Sr. Basic	3,533	5,06,587	2,32,287	7,38,874	27,440
Secondary/Hr. Sec.	3,164	2,24,753	92,343	3,17,096	53,626
Degree, Pre-Degree & Post Grad.	400	1,78,460	37,394	2,15,854	NA
Teacher Training	15	2,708	1,066	3,774	NA
Total	43,951	33,43,553	19,61,269	53,04,822	1,60,450

Source : 'Educational Statistics at a Glance, 1973,' Ministry of Education and Social Welfare, Government of India, New Delhi, 1974.

Establishment of S.V. University

Prior to establishment of S.V. University in 1954, all the Colleges situated in that area were affiliated to Madras University. Later in 1954, according to the Act XIV of 1954 of the Andhra State legislature, S.V. University was inaugurated on September 2, 1954, as a teaching and residential University to start with. The University assumed affiliating functions from the academic year 1956-57. All the colleges in the districts of Nellore, Cuddapah, Kurnool, Anantapur and Chittoor were affiliated to the newly established Sri Venkateswara University, at Tirupati.

Plan	No. of affiliated Colleges	Total
Before 1951	6	6
Plans : I 1951-56	2	8
II 1956-61	1	9
III 1961-69	13	22
IV 1969-74	6	28
V 1974-79	1	29

Survey of S.V. University Area Colleges

Preliminary

Out of 29 affiliated colleges in S.V. University area, only 24 colleges have sent their replies by way of questionnaire. About 10 colleges were visited personally to see the condition of these libraries.

Among 29 colleges, 6 colleges were established before 1951 ; 2 during first plan period ; 1 during second plan ; 13 during third plan ; 6 during fourth plan and only one during the fifth plan period.

Five colleges have also extended evening colleges facilities in degree courses out of 24 colleges in the area 6 colleges are exclusively teaching degree classes and in the rest of the colleges intermediate classes are combined.

Student Strength	*No. of Colleges*
Less than 200	1
Between 250-500	2
Between 501-750	5
Between 750-1000	4
Between 1000-1250	2
Between 1251-1500	3
Above 1500	7
Total	24

Among teaching population, staff position is 16 minimum to 140, maximum depending upon the strength of students. On an average student-staff ratio is 1 : 14. All the 24 colleges have qualified librarians. Most of them are Post Graduates with B. Lib. Sc. degree holders putting not less than 10-15 years of experience. Percentage of library expenditure compared to college expenditure ranges from 1 per cent to 10 per cent.

Management of Library

Out of 24 colleges, only 6 colleges do not have any type of committees to advise the library. In all the colleges where committees are constituted, they are advisory by nature and the committee consists of principal as chairman, 2 or 3 lecturers as members and the librarian as the convenor and member secretary. The main functions of the committee being book selection and budget approval and distribution of funds among various departments.

Out of 24, eight colleges have Professors in-charge apart from qualified librarians.

Library staff

Regarding library staff each college has a minimum of 2, to a maximum of 6 persons. Out of them, 6 colleges have 2 professional staff and in the rest of them only one. Even among two professional one is a professional and the other semi-professional who is designated as Assistant Librarian. Other staff are Record Assts. and Attenders. Every College has, depending upon the strength of the College, 1 to 3 members of non-professionals. Fifteen librarians do possess M.A., B.Lib.Sc. and among Asst. Librarians 5 are B.A. with C.L.Sc. or B.L.Sc.

All the qualified librarians are paid UGC scales as approved by the State Government. Five librarians out of 24 have published articles and four librarians conducted orientation lectures during the beginning of academic year for the benefit of freshers.

Finance

This particular aspect of the questionnaire is most sensitive. Though certain information is furnished, they may not be authentic. Even so many arguments are made by the librarians, when questioned about their difficulty to answer suitably. Firstly relevant records are not maintained properly ; secondly even if a few colleges maintain records, they are unable to give particulars for the past years since it involves more time and tests the patience of an individual ; thirdly in the private management they totally avoid issuing particulars, because they would be committed in writing and also their management will not agree to furnish such correct information. So with all these obstacles certain information was received, but on this basis correct analysis could not be made.

Out of 24 colleges, within a span of 5 years between 1971-75 only 9 colleges got government grants and 7 colleges UGC grants ; 3 colleges both government as well as UGC grants ; that too not for all the years continuously, but used to get sporadically. Besides this, the revenue for the college library is only the library fee collected in three terms on a year, @ Rs. 15/- per annum which is insufficient to meet the requirements of the library. Both the Government and Aided colleges collect library fees or reading room fees. Since there are no proper records which reveal exact resources as well as expenditure, clear cut usage distributing to various items could not be assessed properly. Most of the colleges do spend their meagre resources towards books and periodicals, furniture, and binding unproportionately.

There is no fixed policy with regard to percentage or quantum of expenditure to be met towards each of the most important items (books and periodicals ; furniture and binding). This aspect entirely depends upon the discretion of the principal of the college.

There is no ad hoc or standard policy for acquisition of books. Instead, entire purchases are made at a time during the end of the financial year as against making purchases periodically spreading throughout the academic year.

There is no specifie percentage of expenditure towards current periodicals subscription. Moreover, this expenditure is negligible when compared to that of books.

Building

Though separate well-planned buildings are indispensable for organizing the libraries on modern lines to the entire satisfaction of the users, in this area of college library fields, this statement does not hold good since the majority of college do not have suitable buildings at all.

Out of 24 colleges, 7 colleges have independent buildings ; 11

colleges, a wing of their college building being used as library space : and the remaining colleges have "No man's place" i.e., "safe where we are", satisfied with the space allocated for library accommodation without any area left over for reading rooms.

Irrespective of owning the buildings or not, only 25 percent of the libraries are furnished with reading room space and tables and chairs. Apart from the above furniture wooden cup-boards, man stands and notice-boards are provided. Colleges which have their own separate library buildings are provided with a small counter for issue transaction and a small area for stacks. A separate hall is also provided for reading purposes. Good lighting and ventilation is provided.

Book Collection

Out of 24 colleges, only 10 colleges receive books on donation, besides usual purchases. No college library has any exchange programme of books and periodicals, nor any of the colleges lend books on inter-library loan. Nineteen colleges have UGC text books collection and 14 colleges have established book-banks are stipulated by UGC. The following Table will give an idea of book collection-Number of colleges.

Book stock	Number of Colleges
Less than 1000	—
1000—5000	5
5,001—10,000	4
10,001—20,000	6
20,001—30,000	4
30,001—40,000	3
40,001—50,000	2
Above 50,000	—

With regard to rate of additions every year, out of 24 colleges only 6 colleges acquire or add to the stock more than 1000 books ; 8 colleges more than 500 books : and the rest less than 250 books.

Majority of the libraries acquire text books in multiple copies. About 15 libraries purchase reference books and 12 libraries books of general nature.

Excepting two colleges which subscribe to more than 100 journals, rest of them subscribe as follows : 2 colleges less than 50 journals ; 4 colleges less than 30 journals ; and the rest of the colleges did not reply. Among the colleges which subscribe to journals, 95 per cent of the journals are of Indian origin. Almost all the colleges purchase important Reference Tools, viz, Encyclopaedias, Dictionaries, Directories, Year Books and so on.

Acquisitions

In almost all the colleges, selection precedure is one and the same. i.e., the Heads of Departments select books for their departments and send indents to the librarian. As far as general books are concerned the librarian will select and take the approval of the library committee. In a few instances the principal himself selects general books besides the librarian. No library maintains order cards but instead, maintains files of correspondence. Of late, it is understood that some Heads of Departments are permitted by a few college authorities to make a personal selection of books at city centres along with the librarian. This may, in a way, be a substitute to an indent, in which many books may not be available in the market.

Majority of the colleges do acquire books through their respective co-operative stores, and a few colleges from a local book shop by inviting quotations. Many colleges prefer co-operative stores, because they offer 15 per cent discount in general for all types of books.

In the case of periodicals acquisition, most of the general reading room journals are subscribed with local book-sellers, and in a very few colleges, journals are subscribed with subscription agencies at Bombay, Madras or Hyderabad. No library can afford to subscribe journals directly with the foreign publishers.

In general, the policy procedures mainly depend upon the principal's preferences. Firstly, the colleges wish to have quotations with regard to terms and conditions of supply of books. To avoid audit objections and unnecessary criticism, they prefer only co-operative stores to supply their requirements with maximum discount ranging from 15 to 20 per cent.

Processing

Out of 24 colleges in the area, excepting 5 colleges, rest of the colleges do classify books. All the colleges classify books according to Dewey Decimal Classification Scheme—1 college with 14th Edn. of DDC ; 1 college with 15th Edn. ; 6 colleges with 16th Edn ; 5 colleges with 17th Edn ; 3 colleges with 18th Edn. ; and 3 colleges did not make any particular reference to the number of edition.

Even as for this scheme 5 colleges followed close or depth scheme : 14 colleges broad scheme and only one a simple scheme.

With regard to cataloguing, 11 libraries follow ALA code and the rest do not have particular code. 8 colleges have adopted conventional card catalogue of 5″×3″—and out this 4 colleges type the cards and the rest maintain hand-written card catalogue. 16 colleges followed register method of cataloguing (printed cataloguing).

Most of the colleges classify and catalogue books without area of work but a few colleges which have fallen in backlog do not have or drawn a particular scheme by which it can be cleared.

Circulation and Maintenance

All the colleges do prepare books for circulation by equipping each of the book with ownership mark, date label, spine label etc. Ten libraries out of 24 issue reader's cards maintaining class and roll numbers. Nine libraries maintain register type record assigning few pages for individual borrowers. Six libraries maintain Browne system and one library Newark system and other libraries their own indigenous system. The clientele of the library constitutes students, teachers and ministerial staff of the college. Number of registered borrowers ranges from 200—2000 among students : staff and others range from 20-250. The average daily attendance ranges from 30-500 among students ; 20-85 among the teaching staff and among the rest from 10-23.

Nineteen colleges offer orientation lectures to the new entrants as to the use of the library at the beginning of the academic year. In almost all the libraries the working days and working hours fall in line with the college working hours and days—four colleges work between 9.00 A.M. and 9.00 P.M., four colleges from 9.30 A.M. to 5.00 P.M. and the rest of them between 10.00 A.M. to 4.30 P.M. Only five colleges open their reading rooms on Sundays. All the college libraries extend lending facilities to their clientele (students, and teachers). Students are issued 1-3 books and teachers 10-20 books. Period of loaning of books ranges from 10-15 days for the students, and from one term to no limit for teachers. As far as over-due charges are concerned they are collected from the students, exempting the staff. No library deposit is collected from the students. The average number of books borrowed by teachers ranges from 150-600 ; and for the students it ranges from 50-200 in a year. Except one library the rest of the libraries do not extend inter-library-loan facilities. 50 percent of the libraries put forth their special efforts to promote the library use by arranging talks on library use ; by displaying jackets of new books ; by organising occasional book exhibitions.

Out of 24 colleges, 9 colleges resort to closed access, 3 colleges have partial open access, and the rest of colleges resort to open access. All the colleges do have stock verification annually—one college does stock verification with the help of shelf-list ; two colleges with the help of classified part of the catalogue and the rest with the help of Accession Register. Few more colleges prepare a list of numerical numbers serially from 1 to 5000 or so, depending upon the approximate total number of books and round off the items after checking the Accession Numbers on the books. Accession numbers on the books are initialled by the checking Assistant. The average annual loss of books for five years from 1970-1971 to 1974-75 reveal on an average losses ranging from 20-200 books. Four libraries report less than 10 books toward loss and the only one library states that there was a little scope for loss. In 12 colleges, the library staff are held responsible for loss of books, and 5 colleges insist on security deposit against the risk of losing the books. 50 percent of the colleges do take precautions to prevent losses of books by keeping vigilance at the gate, by way of closed access ; and by collecting penalty for losses. Most of the colleges appoint one attender for cleaning and dusting the library stacks periodically and a few colleges make use of insect killing machines or dust blowing equipment.

Few librarians maintain statistical data up-to-date. The usual statistical records maintained by almost all the librarians are as follows:

1. Borrower's Registers.
2. Issue Registers.
3. Accession Registers.
4. Periodicals Registers.

All the libraries bring out Annual Reports along with the College Administration report, which are published annually.

A very few colleges have plans to construct new buildings exclusively for the library with all facilities needed. The overall issue is with regard to inadequate staff, insufficient space and more book grants. Senior principals of two colleges have suggested their sincere opinion to fulfil the desire to have a functional and service library.

Analysis made on the basis of data obtained reflects in general a gloomy picture of the college administration and organization in our area even with the existing norms and standards which are outdated. The libraries could not attain a good image in the eyes of users. I personally feel that the data gathered so far never give me any perspective on which I can base any norms or standards excepting to draw a few conclusions. I find no new venue or vista on which I can formulate either new theories or suggest fixed norms and standards.

Though there is possibility to fix up standards and norms with qualitative and quantitative analysis using statistical techiques, the entire area cannot be covered. The possible areas that can be taken up may be circulation section, library resources, utilization of funds, staffing pattern, provided correct information as needed in the questionnaire is furnished. In the absence of it that part of standardization cannot be worked out.

Under these circumstances, on the basis of aforesaid analysis, the following observations are found to be a via-media compromise for careful cosideration.

A. 1. The inspection commission of each University should lay down norms for libraries in affiliated colleges, in consultation with the University librarian :

2. At least 6 per cent of the total budget of the college should be allocated to the library. Out of this amount, the college administration should provide 25 per cent and the U.G.C. and the State Government together 75 per cent.

3. The library hours should extend beyond the normal college hours and additional staff should be provided for the purpose.

4. Every year the librarian should conduct as a regular feature, initiation of college students in small batches to the organisational and service aspect of the library during the first term.

5. The present system of class-room oriented education is responsible for the improper use of books, and therefore, reorientation of the existing teaching methods towards more and more library work may be considered.

6. There should be, at periodical intervals, refresher courses to enable the librarians to be up-to-date with the techniques of librarianship.

7. The periodical weeding-out of books should be done preferably once in five years.

8. Students from any college by producing identity cards may be allowed to consult and study in the University Library and in any college library.

9. A system of inter-library loan should be established among colleges in the University area and that the S.V. University Library will be the central-library for co-ordinating and expediting the services.

10. The University should publish a union catalogue of the holdings of each of its affiliated college libraries and maintain it as a means for carrying out an effective inter library loan service.

11. The basic books which are curriculum-related should be acquired in adequate duplicate copies to meet the needs of the students and staff, and therefore, should not be included in the inter-library loan system.

12. The college libraries may participate in book-loan programme of other institutions in India.

13. The Principals of colleges taking into consideration the use of books by the faculty members allow them to borrow books for a specific period without causing any inconvenience to students and other readers.

14. For the effective functioning of lending services both at the university and affiliated colleges level catalogues of exising books and journals should be prepared and exchanged for mutual benefit, and the managements and the government be requested to finance the project.

15. Open access system should be introduced in all the college libraries in spite of loss of books. The cost of books lost may however be written off after thorough enquiry.

16. The Libraries should work from 9 a.m. to 9 p.m. through a properly arranged shift system.

B. 1. Part-time employment should be provided for students under the supervision of the permanent staff for providing extra amenities for the users of the Library.

2. The University library should send lists of current periodicals and journals to the affiliated colleges so that they can be acquired for the college libraries.

3. Library fees may be fixed in such a way that for every Rs. 3/- paid by the student, a similar amount is paid by the management, Rs. 6/- by the State Government and Rs. 12/- by the University Grants Commission as a matching grant. This would mean Rs. 24/- per student which will be a satisfactory amount.

4. The College library authorities may write-off the value of five books at every 1000 books circulated for use.

C. 1. The Librarian has to be put at par with the faculty members in all matters concerning academic work and administration of the Library including emoluments and fringe benefits.

2. The practice of continuing the professor as incharge of the library even when a fully qualified Librarian is appointed may be discontinued forthwith.

3. The Librarians should be given better opportunities to visit larger and well-organised libraries and study their working. Top-ranking Librarians be invited to College Libraries to deliver lectures and advise the librarians and the staff for improvement and efficiency.

4. In regard to the personnel in the College Libraries, there must be one professional and two non-professionals for the first 5000 books and one professional and one non-professional be added for every additional 500 books or part thereof.

5. College Librarians should be deputed to University or other college libraries for learning modern techniques and methods for more effective service, and that the University should provide necessary facilities in carrying out this programme.

6. The Librarians of the college libraries should be allowed to participate in the preparation of the Library Budget.

7. The status of the Library staff should be the same as that of the teaching staff.

8. The conditions of services of the Librarians should be the same as that of Faculty Members.

9. The services of the Librarians should be utilised on the various committees of the University.

10. The required number of Assistants should be provided to the Librarian to enable him to run the Library efficiently.

COLLEGE LIBRARIES IN ANDHRA PRADESH II
Osmania University Area

Libraries constitute a direct incentive to the development of educational social and cultural activities. They contribute immensely to the arousal of public interest in day-to-day affairs by facilitating exchange of knowledge among different sections of people. This goes a long way in annihilating the chief enemies of democracy, apathy and ignorance. In the words of Dr. S.R. Ranganathan, "Libraries are no more store houses ; they are rich springs from which knowledge flows out to irrigate the wide field of education and culture".

Libraries are primarily important because they are reservoirs of knowledge. They are places where research is carried out, the research workers tapping and harnessing the knowledge made available to them. The word research usually conjures up in the mind a picture of a laboratory, with workers in white coats carefully carrying test-tubes ; but, taking all fields of knowledge into consideration, more research is done in libraries than in laboratories Libraries are also powerful contributors to the spread of education. They supplement the work of the teachers and educate and enlighten those who have no teacher.

The importance of the library in the work of schools and colleges is being gradually appreciated. One result of this is the growing demand that the library should be the central feature of the scheme of new school and college buildings. The function of the library in enabling people to educate themselves has long been appreciated. The public library is considered to have played a decisive part in educating them. Libraries are also places where a mine of information can quickly be found on virtually every subject ; the problem confronting the chemist in his experiments ; the problems confronting the boy making his own model aeroplane—these problems have one thing in common, that is, they can be solved by visiting a library.

The contents of libraries not only supply knowledge, but they provide pleasure too. Reading is one of the most popular of the hobbies, and libraries can supply books to suit a variety of tastes. One of the function of the library is to provide pleasure to its valuable clientele by way of making books available for them especially those catering for people, like hospital patients, prisoners and so on.

The importance of libraries has been duly stressed because it needs adequate measure of stressing. Libraries contain books, together with matter supplementing books, such as periodicals. In a nutshell, no substitute could ever be provided for the contents of a library, collectively called "Library Materials".

Library-College

When a college is a library and a library is a college, it is a "Library-College", a term always spelled with a hyphen.

"The purpose of the Library-College", according to the Jamestown Charter, so called after the Jamestown (North Dakota) College Workshop held in December 1965, is to increase the effectiveness of student-learning, particularly through (though not limited to) the use of library-centres, independent study with a bibliographically expert faculty . . . the "Library-College Concept" can and should be adapted to colleges with varying objectives and philosophies.

Library-Colleges is a concept which constitutes and heralds a vigorous movement for promotion of universal education. It is anti-elitist in its philosophy, its avowed objective being "College for All" which is an essential pre-requisite for democracy. History will document that violent revolution is aroused and fostered when the top brass constituting the 10 per cent of the members of the society for whom higher education is reserved exclusively, can no longer communicate and forge contact with the remaining 90 per cent who are denied the privilege of college learning.

The advent of universal higher education has created the widest range of individual differences, and, in the wake of this anomalous situation, it has become all the more imperative to establish a college solely for those who are prevented from gaining access to what is called "Ivory Tower", which is the exclusive privilege of the top brass. The ivory tower approach is highly reprehensible and is to be shed in an egalitarian society.

The widespread library movement and the proliferation of books and reading materials on a vast variety of subjects have brought about a shift from the classroom group teaching to library individual and independent study. This innovation has virtually reversed the relationship between the class-room and library, in that the student resorts to study of books and other reading materials in the library and seldom attends the classes. He is of the opinion that mere class-room teaching does not constitute a solution for the ticklish problems confronting the teacher and the taught. During the course of study in the library, he would be confronted by doubts. As such, he has perforce to approach his teacher to get his doubts cleared.

The Library-College concept has also contributed, not a little, to the attainment of a pre-eminent position by bibliographical study to which a student resorts. It has entirely changed the primitive and out-moded role the teacher was called upon to play. Here, the teacher has to advise the student to resort to intensive study of valuable books available in the library to gain general knowledge and those books which have a vital bearing on the class-room study. It is also incumbent on the part of the teacher to enlighten the student through what is called 'the generic book'.

With the advent of a wide network of audio-visual education coupled with sophisticated computer system and large scale production of printed books and other reading materials containing a mine of relevant and valuable information, it has become possible to provide and custom-tailor communication to the individual differences of student population regardless of range.

The faculty ; bibliographic counsellor ; and the generic book ; the change in curriculum ; workstudy ; each-one—teach-one ; values ; etc., are the factors which are Indispensable for a student vis-a-vis higher education.

Place of College-Library in Education

A College is an institution of higher education which opens to its entrant new vistas of knowledge, inculcates in him a sense of purpose of values, enables him to be responsive and responsible to the problems faced by the contemporary society and motivates him to contribute his mite to the welfare of his fellow beings. The education imparted, therefore, should be meaningful and relevant. A college library takes pride of place in so far as it provides room and gives encouragement to the fulfilment of individual needs and requirements.

The learning which takes place within the four walls of a classroom or laboratory is supplemented and complemented by a variety of resources and competent staff of a really effective library. It is a place which takes an individual to the world of ideas and imagination, acquaints him with the live issuess of life, the sufferings of humanity, the challenges of times and leaves him free to ponder, to decide and to act. In short, it is an agency which tries to take an individual out of the narrow realms of scholasticism and exposes him to the world outside and thus brings to him the benefits of liberal education.

Until very recently, the imparting of instruction in colleges and universities was being done in the traditional way. It was lecture-cum-examination-oriented. There was not much of involvement of the teacher in the teaching process and of the student in the learning process. The teacher was more concerned with 'finishing' the prescribed portion and the student in mugging the required facts and figures. The anomalous two hardly interacted. The college library, in such a situation, could be nothing but an appendage. Fortunately, the times are fast changing.

The introduction of semester system of education is expected to make in-roads into the traditional system by a variety of means and thus allow ample opportunities both for the teacher and the taught to get themselves involved in the entire educational process and make it more meaningful and relevant. The three basic ingredients of the semester education are : (a) its approach, (b) its duration and (c) its method of evaluation, and thus it brings to him the benefits of liberal education.

The role of a college library in semester system of education is of high significance. It needs to be one which actively supports and enlivens and the teaching-learning process by involving closely both the teacher and the taught in the assimilation of knowledge by means of graphic and non-graphic records. The library staff undoubtedly takes a major share of this role. However, it is essentially a co-operative venture. The principal, the teacher, the student and the librarians should lend active support to play their part fully and meaningfully.

Basing on the existing situation in the college libraries, time has come to review and suggest suitable norms and standards and also the system of education—semester, non-semester or traditional—so as to evolve proper modifications in streamlining the organization to deliver the goods to the user to his satisfaction. For this purpose, a survey has been conducted and its analysis is given hereunder.

Let me enumerate and state what exactly are the causes leading to the existence of the dismal situation obtaining in the college libraries. The following are the few, to which proper and tangible solution has to be found and implemented without much delay.

1. The management and the administration alike, have not realised that a library is an integral part of a college since there is confusion as regards the purpose. No conscious effort is ever made for book-provision and its administration.
2. Meagre financial resources.
3. Inadequate library accommodation.
4. Ignoring the essential condition of appointment of a qualified and competent librarian and supporting staff.
5. Out-moded curriculum and method of instruction.
6. Faculty members not evincing interest.
7. Lack of love of reading among the student community.

This sad and unwanted situation, which was observed by me when I personally visited one of the oldest and the richest of the college-libraries in Osmania University area. This prompted me to take up this ambitious project of "Surveying the existing conditions of college libraries in Andhra Pradesh, and to suggest certain standards and norms for adoption with a view to achieving and facilitate effective functioning".

Scope

The present study attempts to reveal the existing condition of college libraries in Andhra Pradesh, with special reference to Osmania University. The emphasis is on "Fact-finding". College libraries, for this purpose, include only arts, science and commerce colleges. For the sake of convenience, clarity and uniformity, the following categories of colleges are excluded.

Medical, Engineering and Polytechnic (Nehru Technological University, Andhra Pradesh), Agriculture and Veterinary (Agricultural University, Andhra Pradesh), and Oriental Colleges. The area under reference is confined to those colleges affiliated to Osmania University situated in Andhra Pradesh.

Educational System

As regards higher education, the State of Andhra Pradesh has three Universities, viz, Osmania University, established in 1918, with jurisdiction over the Telangana region with 9 districts ; the Andhra University, established in 1926, with jurisdiction over coastal Andhra Districts of Sikakulam, Visakhapatnam, East Godavari, West Godavari, Krishna, Prakasam and Guntur and the Sri Venkateswara University, established in 1954, with jurisdiction over the districts of Nellore, Chittoor, Cuddapah, Anantapur and Kurnool. Increase in the number of colleges year after year, coupled with the growing demand for the post-graduates in various sectors of development necessitated the establishment of three post-graduate centres in the State during 1967-78. The three Centres are *Warangal* in Osmania University area, *Guntur* in Andhra University area and *Anantapur* in Sri Venkateswara University area. Of late, during 1976, the two PG Centres, at Warangal attached to Osmania University area ; and Guntur attached to Andhra University area have been upgraded as independent universities named as *Kakateeya University, Warangal* and *Nagarjuna University, Guntur*, respectively. But the PG Centre at Anantapur attached to Sri Venkateswara University area was made Autonomous PG Centre with a Director with the status of Vice-Chancellor.

Each University in the State is both a teaching and an affiliating university. The affiliated colleges, which are managed by the Government, and the private bodies, offer under-graduate courses of study. There are separate colleges for women, and most of the colleges for men are co-educational in character. Evening colleges have also been established for the benefit of employees who could learn while in the process of earning.

The educational system gives an over-all picture of the system of education in vogue in Andhra Pradesh. The nationally recommended 10+2+3 structure has already been introduced in the state. Generally, a child joins the regular stream of schooling at the age of 5 plus. Provision is also available, to some extent, for pre-primary education of children belonging to the age-group 3—4. The primary stage extends to 5 years. This is followed by a two year course of upper primary or middle school education. Thus, the child in the normal course joins a secondary school at the age of 11 plus and takes a three-year course there. The pupil takes a public examination at the end of the course, by which time, he would have reached the age of 15 plus. The Intermediate or Higher Secondary Course offered in the Junior College for Secondary School Leavers is of two years' duration. Students who take to professional course like primary teachers' training, polytechinc, engineering, medical, education etc., divert from the main track of general education just before or after the Intermediate Course. The first degree course is of three years' duration, followed, close on its heels, by a two year-course of MA, MSc, MCom, MSW, MBA etc.

Survey : Preliminary

Out of 84 affiliated colleges in the Osmania University area, only 30 colleges have sent in their replies by way of questionnaire. About 21 colleges were visited personally to observe for myself the condition of those libraries.

Among 84 colleges, 4 colleges were established prior to 1951, 8 during the First Plan Period, 8 during the Second Plan Period, 31 during the third Plan Period, 25 during the Fourth Plan Period and 8 during the Fifth Plan Period, as indicated in the Table 1 :

TABLE 1

Plan period	No. of affiliated colleges	Total
Before 1951	4	4
I 1951-56	8	12
II 1956-61	8	20
III 1961-69	31	51
IV 1969-74	25	76
V 1974-79	8	84

Four colleges have also extended evening college facilities in degree courses in the area. Ten colleges are exclusively teaching degree classes ; one college teaches P.G. course and in the rest of the colleges intermediate classes are combined, as indicated in the Table 2 :

TABLE 2

	Student-strength	No. of colleges
Less than	250	3
Between	250-500	14
	501-750	5
	751-1,000	1
	1,001-1,250	2
	1,251-1,500	3
	1,501	2

Among the teaching population, the staff position is 14 minimum to 110 maximum, depending upon the strength of students and number of departments. On an average, student-staff ratio is 1 : 20. Out of 30 colleges, 15 colleges have qualified librarians and the rest do not have qualified librarians ; 15 qualified librarians are post-graduates with CLSc. They have gained 4-16 years of experience. The percentage of library expenditure, compared to college expenditure ranges from 2 to 12½%.

Management

Out of 30 colleges, 12 colleges do not have any type of committees to advise the library. In all the colleges where committees are constituted, they are advisory by nature, and the Committee consists of the Principal as Chairman and the librarian as the convenor and member-secretary, the main function of the committee being 'book selection' and 'budget approval and distribution of funds' among various departments. Out of 30, 6 colleges have professors or lecturers in charge, apart from qualified librarians.

Library Staff

Regarding library staff, each college has a minimum of one to a maximum of five persons. Out of them, 2 colleges have 2 professionals one is a professional while the other is a semi-professional, designated as Assistant Librarian. Other staff are Record Asst. and Attenders. Every college has, depending upon the strength of the students, staff and books, 1 to 3 non-professionals. Fifteen librarians do posses MA and BLibSc. and among the Asst. Librarians, I post-graduate and 3 post-graduates possess BLibSc or CLSc.

Finance

This particular aspect of the questionnaire is most sensitive. Though certain information is furnished, it may not be authentic. As spate of arguments are given by the librarians, when questioned about their difficulty to answer suitably. Firstly, relevant records are not maintained properly ; secondly, even if a few colleges maintain records, they are unable to give particulars for the past years since it inevitably involves consumption of more time and tests the patience of an individual ; thirdly, in the private management, they totally avoid issuing particulars, presumably because they would have to be committed in writing. What is more, their managements would not agree to furnish such correct information. So, with all these obstacles, certain information was received, but on this basis correct analysis could not be made.

Out of 30 colleges, within a span of 5 years between 1970-75 only 6 colleges got State Government Grants, 9 colleges University Grants Commission Grants, 6 colleges both State as well as University Grants Commission Grants sporadically. The other source of revenue is by way of library fee collected in a year.

There is no specific percentage of expenditure towards current periodicals subscription. Moreover, this expenditure is negligible when compared to that of books.

Building and Furniture

Though, separate, well-planned buildings are indispensable for organizing the libraries on modern lines to the entire satisfaction of the users, in this area of college library field, this statement does not hold good since the majority of the colleges do not have suitable buildings at all.

Out of 30 colleges, only 4 colleges have independent buildings, 7 colleges, a wing of their own college building, and the remaining colleges do not have buildings at all. Seven colleges are contemplating to have separate library buildings.

Seven libraries are using library steel racks and the rest are using wooden racks. Tables and chairs are made of wood. A negligible number of colleges use steel catalogue cabinets and other important fittings required for the library.

Irrespective of whether the buildings are owned or not, only 25 per cent of the libraries are furnished with reading room space and tables, and chairs. Apart from the above furniture, wooden cupboards, map stands and notice boards, are provided. Colleges which have their own separate library buildings are provided with a small counter for issue transaction and a small area for stacks. A separate hall is also provided for reading purposes. Facilities for good lighting and ventilation exist.

Book-collection

Out of 33 colleges, only 5 colleges receive books on donation, besides usual purchases. No college library has launched any exchange programme of books and periodicals nor does any of the colleges lend books on inter-library loan. 19 colleges have University Grants Commission grants book collection. 11 colleges have 'poor students'

—lending facilities and 12 colleges have book banks.

TABLE 3

Book-stock	No. of colleges
Less than 1000	—
1001-5000	10
5001-10000	10
10001-20000	8
20001-30000	2
30001-40000	—
40001-50000	—
50001	—
	30

Rate of Addition

Out of 30 colleges, 3 colleges only add more than 1,000 books to the book-collection ; while 19 colleges get more than 500 books added. Six colleges carry on the process of addition of 250 books. The rest of the college are not engaged in the process.

Most of the colleges acquire text books in multiple copies. Reference books and books of general nature are also purchased.

Only one college subscribes to more than 100 journals while 4 colleges subscribe to less than 50-99 ; 5 colleges procure journals ranging between 30-50, by way of subscription, the remaining colleges subscribe to less than 20 journals.

Acquisitions

In almost all the colleges, the selection procedure is one and the same, i.e., the heads of departments select books for their departments and send in indents to the librarians. As far as general books are concerned, the librarian will select and take the approval of the library committee. In a few instances, the principal himself, besides the librarian, selects general books. No library maintains order cards but instead, they maintain files of correspondence. It is understood that, of late, some heads of departments are permitted by a few college authorities to make a personal selection of books at City Centres along with the librarian. This may, in a way, be a viable alternative in preference to the method of indenting for books, in as much as in the latter case, the possibility of non-availability of many books in the market is not ruled out. Personal selection, constitutes, by far, the best and viable alternative.

Majority of the colleges do acquire books through their respective co-operative stores, while a few colleges procure them from local bookshops by way of inviting quotations. Many colleges prefer co-operatives stores in view of the fact that the latter offer 15 per cent discount, in general, for all types of books.

In the case of periodicals, most of the general reading room journals are subscribed to and procured from local booksellers, and in a very few colleges, journals are subscribed to and procured from subscription agencies at Bombay, Madras and Hyderabad. No library can afford to subscribe to journals directly and procure them from the foreign publishers.

In general, the policy procedures mainly depend upon the Principal's preferences. Firstly, the colleges wish to have quotations with regard to terms and conditions of supply of books. With a view to avoiding audit objections and undue criticism, they prefer only co-operative stores for supply of their requirements with maximum discount ranging from 15 to 20 per cent.

The acquisition of books are made through :

Library Committee	7 colleges
By Heads of Departments	22 colleges
Individual recommendation	13 ,,
Librarians' recommendation (Gen. Books)	17 ,,
Direct purchase by authorities	10 ,,

Processing

Out of 30 colleges in the area, the following is the break-up of classification system : 16 colleges carry on the process of clasifying books. While 4 colleges do not undertake classification work, 5 colleges have not responded in the matter.

The pertinent details in regard to pattern of classification adopted by the colleges in the area are given below :

Classification by	
16th ed. DDC	7 colleges
17th ed. DDC	3 ,,
18th ed. DDC	5 ,,

Indigenous system is in vogue in the rest of the colleges. Colon classification is not at all used.

10 colleges adopt DDC broad classification.

4 colleges adopt close classification.

Ten colleges follow ALA Catalogue Code and the catalogue in register from. Only 6 colleges follow conventional card catalogue and even among them only one college used typed cards and the rest use hand-written ones. In general, all the colleges do maintain catalogue in one form or the other. 5 colleges follow dictionary type and 3 colleges employ classified part. Five colleges have a backlog of catalogue work.

Circulation and Maintenance

The following are the relevant particulars as the pattern in vogue in the colleges in the area :

Register method	12 colleges
Reader Cards	5 ,,
Brownie system	5 ,,
Newark system	2 ,,

The following are the details as regards membership :

Students	: 200-2000
Staff and others	: 20-250

Average attendance per day

Students	: 20-80
Rest	: 10-25

Other Details

Twelve colleges do give orientation-lecture at the beginning of the year.

Working Hours :

10 colleges : College working hours.

6 colleges : 9-30 a.m to 5.00 p.m.

Rest of the Colleges : Twice with lunch-break between 1 p.m. and 2 p.m.

Students are issued 2 books between 10-15 days.

Teachers are issued 10-20 with no time limit.

Deposit is collected in a few colleges.

Number of books borrowed in a year by teachers ranges : 150-600.

Number of books borrowed in a year by students ranges : 50-200.

The practice of inter-library loan is not in vogue. Out of 25 colleges, only 7 colleges resort to open access ; while 10 colleges employ closed access. The rest of the colleges adopt partial accesess.

All the colleges do have stock verification annually ; 15 colleges by accession register ; 2 colleges by shelf-list ; and the remaining colleges by some other method of stock verification.

The average annual loss is between 20-200 books. In 13 colleges, the librarian is held responsible for the loss of books. Only 5 colleges stipulate payment of security.

50 per cent of the librarians keep vigilance at the gate.

Miscellaneous

A few librarians maintain statistical data up-to-date. The usual statistical records maintained by almost all the librarians are as follows :

(a) Borrowers' Registers.
(b) Issue Registers.
(c) Accession Registers.
(d) Periodicals checking Registers.

All the libraries bring out Annual Reports along with the college administration reports, and they are published anually.

FUTURE PLAN

A few colleges have plans to construct new buildings exclusively for the library with all the facilities needed. The overall issue is with regard to inadequate staff, insufficient space, and lack of adequate funds.

Suggestions for Standardization

1. The inspection commission or university development committee should lay down norms and guide-lines for scrupulous compliance by the libraries in affiliated colleges, in consultation with the University Librarian.

2. At least 6 per cent of the total budget of the college should be allocated to the library and out of this amount, the college adminis-

tration should provide 25 per cent and the UGC and the state government together 75 per cent.

3. The practice currently in vogue of continuing the professor-incharge of the library, even when a fully qualified librarian is appointed and posted, be discontinued forthwith.

4. There should be standardization in designating the staff employed in all colleges. For this the UGC's advice may be followed.

5. The college librarians should maintain two separate registers mainly for the grants received from two sources, viz. UGC and State (Management). The expenditure should be categorised distinctly under : staff, books and back volumes, periodicals, furniture and fittings, binding, etc. This would enable for the accountability of expenditure for each library and to assess the percentage under each category.

6. A separate library building for housing the books should be built with basic comforts leaving sufficient space for stack-cum reading area and periodicals reading room. Place for the Librarian and other Technical Staff for processing should also be provided with minimum area. Main counter should have a prominent position in the planning of the Library. Measurement for different areas should be worked out taking into account the number of students, teachers and also potential users and visitors. Each building should be equipped with minimum furniture besides library stacks.

7. Basic reference books and text books should find first place among the collection. Comprehensive collection of books should be housed. Rate of addition may be such as should satisfy the objectives of the college library. A minimum of 1000 books covering all the disciplines should be added annually.

8. The heads of departments should suggest minimum number of periodicals related to respective departments for subscription. At least two standard journals for each discipline should be subscribed, besides general reading room periodicals.

9. No time should be lost in the process of acquisition. There should not be many restrictions in acquiring the books. Particularly in academic libraries, the selection process should be vested with the heads of departments as far as subject books are concerned and for general books, the librarian can select and obtain approval of the library committee.

10. There should be uniformity in the scheme of classification and rules of cataloguing for the books processed in all the colleges

affiliated to particular university. This will facilitate compilation of union catalogue. It would be desirable and beneficial if the same assistant prepares catalogue slips, classifies and files the cards to avoid monotonous nature of work of doing the same work all through.

11. Depending upon the strength of students, staff and users, a suitable method of charging system should be adopted.

12. Students and teachers should be issued cards for borrowing books, taking into account the need and size of collection of books.

13. There would be annual stock verification of books for the libraries having less than 20,000 books, whereas for the other libraries with more stock, the verification may be done once in two or three years. Stock taking should be done inevitably with the help of shelf-list cards than the accession register, which should not be spoiled with initials and tick marks.

14. Losses are inevitable, but to avoid losses, proper devices should be introduced. The librarian alone should not be held responsible for the loss as it is the collective responsibility of staff. Certain percentage of losses be accepted due to the circumstances under which a library functions.

15. Periodic weeding out of books that are found to be useless should be done, preferably once in five years to gain shelf space.

16. A system of inter-library-loan should be established among the colleges in the university area and its Central Library, for close coordination and expediting the services. One should act as a liaison to the other.

17. Colleges with more than 10,000 book stock should be thrown open with 'Open Access' and less than that with 'Closed Access'.

18. Payment of security amount by the library staff should be dispensed with, if any.

19. Necessary security staff should be given to keep vigilance at the exit gate.

20. To make the new students to be acquainted with the usage of library, the librarian should organise an orientation lecture every year at the beginning of the session, either collectively or in individual departments, for an hour or two giving demonstration of usage of catalogue, classification and other relevant materials.

21. The present system of class-room-oriented education is responsible for the inadequate use of the library and therefore, there is need for re-orientation of the existing teaching methods with emphasis on greater use of the library.

22. Students from any college, on production of identity card (issued by their respective colleges), may be allowed to consult and study books etc., in any other college or university libraries.

23. All the constituent and affiliated colleges should prepare an extra main entry of catalogue card, for the books that are procured and processed (classified & catalogued) in their library, and send to the University Library to which the college is affiliated, for maintaining a 'union catalogue' in the area, which will serve as a means of carrying out an effective and viable inter-library-loan service.

24. The rules framed by individual library of the college should be implemented sincerely by the staff and seriously observed by the users, for effective functioning of the library.

COLLEGE LIBRARIES IN ANDHRA PRADESH III

Andhra University

At the beginning of 1977 there were 105 Universities, 10 institutions, "deemed to be Universities", 9 institutions of "National importance", empowered to award degrees. In 1975-76 there were 4,508 colleges (of which 3,257 were arts, science and commerce colleges): all affiliated to one University or the other, in India.

The position of the affiliated colleges—especially, the arts and science colleges—in relation to Universities and the Governments makes an interesting subject of study, particularly in the wake of some recent enactments and rules made or proposed to be made for purposes of rendering or withholding of financial assistance to affiliated colleges. Some of the pertinent questions that arise when people consider the problems of financing the private colleges are : Do we need so many private colleges ? ; How much control should government and university exercise over these colleges ? ; What conditions should they fulfil before they become entitled to government grants ?

As the primary function of the university was to lay down syllabuses of study and to examine candidates who appeared for its examinations, these examinations acquired undue importance in the educational process and the inherent tendency of the Indian student to memorize what he reads was given greater impetus. As new colleges came into existence at a fairly rapid rate, especially in places far away from the large cities, the quality of teaching came to be adversely affected. Library facilities were poor, and consequently the students and the teachers read very little, save the textbooks prescribed. The student from a mofussil college had to travel a long distance to appear for the university examinations.

As seen in the early days of the advent of the Indian universities, the affiliated institutions were not purely higher educational institutions. Many colleges had junior and senior sections. The process of affiliation to the University entailed mere sending up of candidates for the examinations of the University. Gradually, the high school and college parts were separated ; and the term "College" came to be used exclusively for the institutions that prepared candidates for the University examinations. But we shall have a few institutions in which the school and college departments are housed together in one set of buildings on one campus.

There has been a steady growth in the number of colleges in most parts of the country. Since the establishment of the first University, the private colleges gradually outnumbered the Government colleges. In fact the growth of Universities and colleges in the country in the last two to three decades in spite of the Five-Year Plans, has been indiscriminate and haphazard.

The increase in the number of affiliated colleges also has taken place for more or less similar reasons. Of the 4,508 affiliated colleges in the country, a vast majority are private institutions established by religious or caste groups or local bodies and societies. In several cases the initial impetus for the establishment of a college has been the long cherished desire of a group of community to have "a finger in the educational pie." Many of these new institutions are wholly dependent on government grants."

The position of the private affiliated college is rather precarious, so to speak. Although many of them are pioneering institutions and have carried the torch of higher education for pretty long time still government and Universities have been inclined to treat them in a step-motherly fashion. It must be admitted on all hands, that some of the newer colleges which came into being without adequate financial resources of their own have the dubious distinction of having recourse to reprehensible methods of raising money and indulging in malpractices such as collecting "capitation fee" from a student as a condition for admission, and extorting money in the garb of 'donations' from teachers as a condition for appointment on the staff. The buildings and equipment of some of these colleges are of very inferior and coarse quality and the standards of teaching and the general behaviour of students and teachers are woefully low. But it is not fair and proper to tar all the colleges with one and the same brush. Some of the difficulties of affiliated colleges arise from lack of freedom—academical and financial. In recent years governments have been inclined to interfere in the affairs of universities and colleges and have used their law-making and grant giving powers to regiment the colleges......a trend which is not a desirable one and amounts to robbing Peter to pay Paul.

Let me enumerate and state what exactly are the causes leading to the existence of the unhappy situation in the college libraries. The following are the few, to which proper and tangible solution has to be found and implemented without much delay.

(i) The management and the administration alike, have not realised that a library is an integral part of a college since there is confusion as regards the purpose. No conscious effort is ever made for book-provision and its administration.

(ii) Meagre financial resources.

(iii) Inadequate library accommodation.

(iv) Ignoring the essential condition of appointment of a qualified and competent librarian and supporting staff.

(v) Curriculum and method of instruction.

(vi) Faculty members not evincing interest.

(vii) Lack of love of reading among the student community.

This sad and unwanted situation, which was observed by me when I personally visited one of the oldest and the richest of the college libraries in the University area, prompted me to take up this ambitious project of "Surveying the existing conditions of College Libraries in Andhra Pradesh and to suggest certain standards and norms for adoption with a view to achieve and facilitate effective and efficient functioning."

Scope

The present study attempts to reveal the existing condition of college libraries in Andhra Pradesh. The emphasis is on 'Fact-finding'. College Libraries, for this purpose, include only arts, science and commerce colleges. For the sake of convenience, clarity and uniformity, the following categories of colleges are excluded :

Medical, Engineering and Polytechnic (Nehru Technological University, Andhra Pradesh), Agriculture and Veterinary (Agricultural University, Andhra Pradesh) and Oriental Colleges. The area under reference is confined to colleges affiliated to Shri Venkateswara, Andhra and Osmania Universities situated in Andhra Pradesh.

Educational System

As regards higher education, the State of Andhra Pradesh has three Universities, viz., Osmania University, established in 1918, with jurisdiction over the Telangana region with 9 Districts, the Andhra University, established in 1926, with jurisdiction over coastal Andhra Districts of Srikakulam, Visakhapatnam. East Godavari, West Godavari, Krishna, Prakasam and Guntur, and the Shri Venkateswara University established in 1954, with jurisdiction over the districts of Nellore, Chittoor, Cuddapah, Anantapur and Kurnool. Increase in the number of colleges year after year, coupled the growing demand for the post-graduates in various sectors of development necessitated to establishment of three Post-Graduate Centres in the State during 1967-78. The three centres are Warangal in Osmania University area. Guntur in Andhra University area and Anantapur in Shri Venkateswara University area.

Each University in the State is both a teaching and an affiliating University. The affiliated colleges, which are managed by the Government and the private bodies, offer undergraduate course of study. There are separate colleges for women, and most of the colleges for men are co-educational in character. Evening colleges have also been established for the benefit of employees who could learn while in the process of earning.

The educational system gives an overall picture of the system of education in Andhra Pradesh. The nationally recommended 10+2+3 structure has already been introduced in the State. Generally, a child joins the regular system of schooling at the age of 5 plus. Provision is also available, to some extent, for pre-primary education of children belonging to the age-group 3-4. The primary stage extends to 5 years. This is followed by a two-year course of upper primary or middle school education. Thus, the child in the normal course joins a secondary school at the age of 11 plus and takes a three-years course there. The pupil takes a public examination at the end of the course, by which time, he would have reached the age of 15 plus. The Intermediate or Higher Secondary course offered in the Junior College for Secondary School leavers is of two years' duration. Students who take to professional course like primary teachers' training, polytechnic, engineering, medical, education, etc., divert from the main track of general education just before or after the Intermediate course. The first degree course is of three years' duration, followed, close on its heels, by a two year-course of M.A., M.Sc., M.Com., or M.B.A.

Survey : Preliminary

Out of 96 affiliated colleges in Andhra University area only 51 colleges have sent in their replies by a questionnaire. About 21 colleges were visited by me with a view to seeing and ascertaining the working conditions prevailing in those libraries.

Among 96 colleges, 20 colleges were established prior to 1951, 11 colleges during the First Five-Year Plan period, only one during the Second Plan Period, 32 colleges during the Third Plan Period, 18 during the Fourth Plan Period and 8 during the Fifth Plan Period. For 6 colleges the date of establishment is not known.

TABLE 1

Plan Period	No. of Affiliated Colleges	Total
Prior to 1951	20	—
I Plan—1951-56	11	31
II Plan—1956-61	1	32
III Plan—1961-66 (69)	32	64
IV Plan—1969-74	18	82
V Plan—1974-79	8	90
Period unknown	6	96

Five colleges have extended Evening College facilities in degree courses. Among the day colleges, 14 colleges are teaching exclusively degree classes, 2 colleges teach P.G. courses and in the rest of the colleges Intermediate and degree courses are combined.

The distribution of the student-population among the colleges is as follows :

TABLE 2

Student Strength	No. of Colleges
Less Than 250	4
Between 251— 500	10
501— 750	4
751—1,000	9
1,001 —1,250	3
1,251—1,500	8
1,501 and above	10
No reply	3
Total	51

With regard to teaching population, the staff position is between the minimum of 10 and the maximum of 142 teachers, depending upon the strength of students, types of courses and number of departments. On an average, the staff-student ratio is 1 : 14.

Management of College Libraries

Out of 51 colleges, 39 colleges have library committees, and student participation is involved in 22 committees. College Librarians are members in only 21 Committees for each of the College Committees, wherever they exist. The Principal functions as Chairman and the College Librarian as Member-Secretary. Wherever Committees are constituted, they are all advisory in nature, and the members are nominated by the Principal, the main function of the Committee being book-selection, budget approval and distribution of funds among various departments. In ten colleges Professors are incharge of libraries, besides the qualified librarians.

Library Staff

Regarding library staff, each college library has a minimum of one to a maximum six persons. Out of 51 colleges 46 have qualified librarians and the rest do not have librarians at all. Sixteen librarians are Post-Graduates with Diploma/Bachelors degree in Lib.Sc. and 20 are graduates with B.Lib.Sc. Among the Assistant Librarians one is a Post-Graduate with Dip/B.Lib.Sc. and the rest are graduates+B.Lib.Sc. Very few Assistant Librarians (who are designated as such by college managements) are Intermediate certificate-holders with C.L.Sc. Most of the librarians have put in 2-26 years of experience. The other staff are Record Assistants, Attenders and peons. Every college Library has 1-3 non-professional depending upon the strength of students, lectures and stock of books. Space and service are not at all considered for additional qualified staff. All the qualified librarians are paid University Grants Commission scales, as approved by the State Government.

Finance

This particular aspect of the questionnaire is most sensitive. Though certain information is furnished, it may not be authentic. A spate of arguments are made by the librarians, when questioned about their difficulty to answer suitably. Firstly, relevant records are not maintained properly; secondly, even if a few colleges maintain records, they are unable to give particulars for the past years since it inevitably involves consumption of more time and tests the patience of an individual ; thirdly, in the private management, they totally avoid issuing particularly, presumably because they would not agree to furnish correct information. So, with all these obstacles certain information was received, but on this basis correct analysis could not be made.

Out of 51 colleges, 14 colleges got State Government Grants, within a span of five years between 1970-75, 19 colleges received University Grants Commission grants and the rest of the colleges could not furnish information. The other sources of revenue comprise donations and library fees ; fine and deposits. University Grants Commission's Grants are, no doubt, received regularly, but they are got sporadically. Besides this, the sole source of a revenue for a library is the library fee collected in three terms in a year, Rs 15/-per annum, which is grossly insufficient to meet the requirements of the library. Both the Government and aided Colleges collect library fees or reading room fees. Since proper records are not maintained which can reveal the exact resources as well as expenditure position, clear-cut usage, distributing among various items could not be assessed properly. Most of the colleges do spend their meagre resources towards purchase of books and periodicals, furniture and binding in an extremely haphazard and slipshod manner.

There is no set policy with regard to percentage or quantum of expenditure to be met towards each of the most important item (books and periodicals ; furniture and binding). This aspect entirely depends upon the discretion of the principal of the college.

There is no ad-hoc and standard policy for acquisition of books. Bulk purchases are made at a time during the end of the financial year as against the usual practice of making purchases periodically spread over the academic year.

There is no specific percentage of expenditure towards current periodicals subscription. Moreover, this expenditure is negligible when compared to that of books.

Building and Furniture

Though separate, well-planned buildings are indispensable for organizing the libraries on modern lines to the entire satisfication of the users, in this area of college library field, this statement does not hold good since the majority of the college do not have suitable buildings at all.

Out of 51 colleges, only seven colleges have independent library buildings. In 19 colleges, libraries are located in one of the halls of the College. Most of the Government Colleges which have their own buildings, have provided 4 to 8 spans of big halls exclusively for libraries. The remaining colleges house their libraries 'in no man's land'.

Excepting seven colleges, the rest of the colleges have, in their libraries both wooden and steel almirahs and racks, reading tables, chairs and display boards. Only eight college libraries have wooden catalogue cabinets for maintaining catalogue cards.

Irrespective of whether the buildings are owned or not, only 25 per cent of the libraries are furnished with reading room space and tables and chairs. Apart from the above furniture, wooden cupboards, map stands and notice boards, are provided. College which have their own separate library buildings are provided with a small counter for issue transaction and a small area for stacks. A separate hall is also provided for reading purposes. Facilities for good lighting and ventilation exist.

Book-collection

Out of 51 colleges, only 21 colleges received books on donation besides usual purchases. Twelve colleges did not receive book on donation at all. Twelve colleges did not furnish any information. No college library has only book-exchange programmes of books and periodicals. Nor does it lend books on inter-library loan. Twenty five colleges have University Grants Commission Text-book collection ; 15 colleges have poor students book-lending scheme. There are no book banks in any of the colleges in the strictest sense.

TABLE 3

Book Stock		No. of Colleges
Less than	1,000	2
Between	1,001—5,000	15
	5,001—10,000	8
	10,001—20,000	4
	20,001—30,000	8
	30,001—40,000	4
	40,001—50,000	1
Above	50,001	—
No information furnished		9
	Total	51

Annual rate of addition of book is as follows :

More than 1,000 books	11 colleges
" 500 books	9 "
" 200 books	8 "

No response was received from the rest of the colleges.

Majority of the colleges acquire text-books in multiple copies. A few latest editions of standard reference books and books of general nature are also acquired.

All the 51 colleges subscribe to current periodicals by way of annual subscription. The following is the break-up.

More than 100 journals	5 Colleges
" 50 "	6 "
" 20 "	15 "
Less than 19 "	6 "

There was no response from the rest of the colleges.

Acquisitions

In almost all the colleges, the selection procedure is one and same, i.e., the Heads of Departments selects books for their departments and send in indents to the librarians. As far as general books are concerned, the librarian will select and take the approval of the library committee. In few instances, the principal himself, besides the librarian, selects general books. No library maintains order cards but, instead, they maintain files of correspondence. It is understood that, of late, some heads of departments are permitted by a few college authorities to make a personal section of books at City Centres along with the librarian. This may, in a way, be a viable alternative in preference to the method of indenting for books, in as much as in the latter case, the possibility of non-availability of many books in the market is not ruled out. Personal selection, constitutes, by far, the best and viable alternative.

Majority of the colleges do acquire books through their respective co-operative stores, while a few colleges procure them from a local bookshop by way of inviting quotations. Many colleges prefer co-operative stores, in view of the fact that the latter offer 15 per cent discount in general, for all types of books.

In the case of periodicals, most of the general reading room journals are subscribed to and procured from local book-sellers, and in a very few colleges, journals are subscribed to and procured from subscription agencies at Bombay, Madras and Hyderabad. No library can afford to subscribe to journals directly and procure them from the foreign publishers.

In general, the policy procedures mainly depend upon the principal's preferences. Firstly, the colleges wish to have quotation with regard to terms and conditions of supply of books. With a view to avoiding audit objections and undue criticism, they prefer co-operative stores for supply of their requirements with maximum discount ranging from 15 to 20 per cent.

Through Library Book-Selection Committee	12	colleges
Heads of Departments	32	,,
Individuals' recommendation	16	,,
Librarian's recommendation	29	,,
Direct selection at bookshops	10	,,

Processing

Out of the 51 colleges in the area, the following is the break-up of classification system.

30 colleges do classify books in one scheme or the other. Eleven colleges do classify for want of classification schedules.

According to DC System	16th	Edition	5	colleges
	17th	,,	11	,,
	18th	,,	8	,,
According to CC System	6th	,,	2	,,

No edition of DC is mentioned by six colleges.

No response is forthcoming from the rest of the colleges.

18 college libraries follow broad classification of DC.

9 college libraries follow depth classification.

With regard to cataloguing of books, 27 colleges adopt Register form of cataloguing and 12 colleges card form of catalogue. The rest of the colleges follow the indigenous form of catalogue to their convenience.

Most of the colleges classify and catalogue books without leaving arrears of work, but a few colleges which may cause backlog do not have a scheme worth the name, they have not drawn up any scheme by means of which the backlog could be wiped out.

Circulation and Maintenance

All the colleges do prepare books for circulation by equipping each of the book with ownership mark, date, labels, spine label, etc. Five libraries, out of 51 issue Reader's cards maintaining class and roll numbers. Twenty six college libraries maintain register type, assigning a few pages for individual borrowers, 3 libraries following Browine system and two libraries Newark system and the rest of the libraries feel satisfied with their own indigenous system of issue and return of books.

The clientele of the library constitute students, teachers and the ministerial staff of the college. The number of registered borrowers range from 100-2,000 among students ; staff and others range between 20-400. The average daily attendance range from 50-300 among the students ; 20-60 among the staff ; and 10-30 among others.

In almost all the libraries the working days and working hours fall in line with the college working hours and days—8 colleges work between 9.30 a.m. and 5.00 p.m. ; 11 colleges between 9.00 a.m. and 9.00 p.m., and the rest of them between 10.00 a.m. and 4.30 p.m.

All the college libraries extend lending facilities to their clientele (students and teachers). Students are issued 1-3 books and teachers 10 to 25. The period of loan of books ranges from 7-15 days for the students and from term to no-limit for teachers. Twenty five libraries issue short term loan of books. In 25 libraries issue days are fixed for different classes in a week ; in 21 libraries books were issued twice a week.

Almost all the libraries collect fine from students whereas the teachers are exempted from overdues. About 19 college libraries collect deposits for loaning the books. The average number of books borrowed by teachers ranges from 700 to unlimited number, and by students between 20 to 1,000 in a year. Only 3 colleges out of 51 extend inter-library-lending facilities. Fifty per cent of the libraries put forth their special efforts to promote the library use by arranging talks on library use, display of book jackets of the new arrivals ; and conduct occasional book exhibitions.

Out of 51 colleges, 18 resort to closed access, 10 colleges partial access and 14 colleges open access. All the colleges do have stock verification of books annually. Six colleges verify with shelf lists ; all 11 colleges do this item of work with the help of library classified part of the catalogue, 24 colleges with the help of accession register and the rest of the colleges in their own way which they find convenient and suitable. Some colleges prepare a list of numerical numbers serially from 1 to 5,000 depending upon the number of books available in the library and round off the items after checking with reference to the accession numbers on the books. Aecession numbers on the book is initialled by the checking assistant.

The average annual loss of books for five years from 1970-71 to 1974-75 reveal, on an average, 20-?00 books. Seventeen libraries reported losses between 10-50 books year. In 16 colleges, the library staff are held responsible for loss of books and 36 colleges accept the loss as inevitable. According to the survey report, no college library has reported about the insistence of security deposit against loss of books. Fifty per cent of the colleges do take precautionary measures to prevent loss of books by keeping vigilance at the gate, by way of closed access and collection of penalty.

Most of the colleges have one Attender (peon) for cleaning and dusting the library stacks and reading tables and a few collegs make use of insect-killing machines or dust-blowing equipment.

Miscellaneous

Few Librarians maintain statistical data up-to-date. The usual statistical records maintained by almost all the librarians are as follows :

(a) Borrowers record.
(b) Issue record.
(c) Accession record.
(d) Periodicals record.

All the libraries bring out Annual Reports along with the college administration reports, and they are published annually.

Future Plan

A few colleges have plans to construct new buildings exclusively for the library with all the facilities needed. The overall issue is with regard to inadequate staff, insufficient space, and lack of adequate funds.

Conclusion

The analysis made on the basis of the data obtained reflects, in general, a gloomy picture of the college administration and organization in our area even with the existing norms and standards which are outdated. The libraries could not portray themselves well and project a brilliant image to their valuable clientele. I personally feel that the data gathered so far never gives me any perspective on which I can base any norms or standards excepting to draw a few conclusions. I find no new venue or vista on which I can formulate either new theories to suggest fixed norms and standards.

Though there is desirability to fix up standards and norms, with qualitative and quantitative analysis using statistical techniques, the entire area cannot be covered. The possible areas that can be taken up may be, circulation section, library resources, utilization of funds, staffing pattern, provided correct and authentic information as needed in the questionnaire is furnished. In the absence of it that part of standardization cannot be worked out.

Under these circumstances, on the basis of the aforesaid analysis the following observations are found to be a via-media compromise for careful consideration.

1. The inspection commission of each University should lay down norms and guidelines for scrupulous compliance by the libraries in affiliated colleges, in consultation with the University Librarian.

2. At least 6 per cent of the total budget of the college should be allocated to the library. Out of this amount, the college administration should provide 25 per cent and the University Grants Commission and the State Government, together 75 per cent.

3. The library hours should extend beyond the normal college hours and additional staff should be provided for the purpose.

4. Every year, the librarian should follow, as a regular feature initiation of college students, in batches, into the organizations and service aspects of the library during the first term.

5. The present system of class-room-oriented education is responsible for the improper use of books, and, therefore, reorientation of the existing teaching methods towards more and more library work may be considered.

6. There should be, at periodical intervals, refresher courses to enable the librarians to be up-to-date with the techniques of Librarianship.

7. Periodic weeding-out of books should be done, preferably once in five years.

8. Students from any college, on production, of identity cards, may be allowed to consult and study books, etc., in the University Library and in any college Library.

9. A system of inter-library loan should be established among the colleges in the University area and its Central Library for close-

co-ordination and expediting the services. One should act as a liaison to the other.

10. The University should publish a union catalogue of the holdings of each of its affiliated college libraries and maintain it as a a means of carrying out an effective and viable inter-library loan service.

11. The basic books which are curriculum-related should be acquired in adequate duplicate copies to meet the needs of the students and staff alike, and hence will not be included in the inter-library loan system.

12. The College libraries may participate in book loan programme of other institutions in India.

13. The Principals of colleges, taking into consideration the use of books by the faculty members, allow them to borrow books for specific period without causing any inconvenience to students and other readers.

14. For the effective and efficient functioning of lending services both at the University and affiliated colleges level catalogue of existing books and journals should be prepared and exchanged for mutual benefit, and the managements and the government be requested to finance the project.

15. In spite of loss of books, open access system should be introduced in all college libraries. The cost of books lost may, however, be written off after a thorough enquiry.

16. The libraries should work from 8 a.m. to 8 p.m. through properly arranged shift system.

17. The practice, currently in vogue of continuing the professor be in charge of the library even when a fully qualified Librarian is appointed and posted may be discontinued forthwith.

ROUND THE LIBRARIES

East Germany

From 14th to 16th Jan. '81, I was taken to the Humboldt University Central Library and introduced to its director (Chief Librarian) Dr. (Mrs.) Viscount Innserem. Having had discussions with her in detail about my aim and purpose of my visit, I was introduced to two more Deputy Directors by name Dr. Kruger who is incharge of processing and questions section and the other Dr. Paul incharge of cataloguing and reading room sections, taken round the library and showed almost all the sections. Next day detailed discussions were held on the areas visited. I also visited the Foreign language section of the Humboldt University and the department of Pedagogics (Education) and department of Mathematics.

During the next week from 20th to 23th Jan. '81, Mr. Muller one of the staff members of the Institute of Library Science of the Humboldt University took me to the Deutsche Stasts Bibliothek (German State Library) and introduced to Mr. Peter Genzil the Deputy Director, incharge of the Acquisitions section. This is one of the Apex Public Library of the country in East Germany which caters to the needs of cross section of the community. Apart from the four main divisions of the library viz 1. Department of Acquistions, 2. Department of Catalogues, 3. Department of Readers Services and 4. Department of Inter lending and union catalogues ; eight more subsections as mentioned below are housed in the same building ; (a) Map Section (b) Music Section (c) Asian-African studies (d) Incunabula section (e) Manuscripts (f) Department of Children and Youth (g) Department of rare and previous books (h) Reprographic section.

At the end of my visit on the last day, I was taken to the Deputy Director General Dr. Gitting who received me on behalf of the Director General and had detailed and fruitful discussion. He had expressed his desire to have exchange of publications between S.V. University and German State Library. (Total collection of books 7 million, Staff-347, Journals on subscription more than 10 thousand.)

28th to 30th January, 81 : Visit to Methodical Centre for Scientific libraries and information and documentation Research. This institute was established in 1965 under the Ministry of Higher Education. This Institute is responsible for the following tasks.

(a) Long term work for the development of libraries.

(b) Policy making, Basic norms and Analysis and Research.

(c) For management of planning state libraries.

(d) Preparing of Decision making to the Ministry.

(e) To Co-ordinate between the Library & Information work.

(f) Specialization for data processing, library construction and Technology.

(g) Collect experiences for Academic libraries and popularize them.

(h) Research work in special fields like, works organization, library Technology, Rationalization work ; and for management.

(i) Long term programme for computerisation.

(j) Organisation of further education (seminars, conferences and workshops).

There is another centre for further education at GOTHA near JENA South East to G.D.R., where original manuscripts are available.

Dr. Gerhard Schwarz, Directer of the Institute arranged for my lecture to address their staff members on comparative study of libraries, in India and G.D.R.

Visited the institute, called Hochschule fur Okonomie (High School for economics) Library as arranged by Humboldt University. Met Dr. Roiswitha Reimer the Director of the Library. This college is the central administration of economy and Foreign Trade ;

companies and prices. This institute is specialized in the following :

(a) Socialist national economics ;

(b) Industrial economics ;

(c) Foreign Trade ;

(d) Statistical and Mathematical Economics (Data processing)

(e) Management of Public Services (Special economics, Public transport construction etc.).

Taken to Berlin City Library (Public) and introduced to Mr. Mayer, Deputy Director of the Library and also to Mrs. Peters, Interpretor. This library comes under the Public Library System. This was established in 1901 for the public by the Town Council. This was actually founded by the working class people and most of the books are gifted by learned men and working class, firms and trade unions. This is the lending centre for public library and also a central lending library. The construction of the new building was begun in 1960, and was completed in 1966 with an up-to-date modern scientific equipment. This library has more than one million and twenty thousand books. This library possesses the following special collection :

(a) History of Berlin ;

(b) Papers of Central Parliament and talks of politicians ;

(c) Literature on German Revolution of 1848-49 ;

(d) Political posters and pamphlets of various parties.

There are special departments like painting, photography, gramophone records (Music library) ; Medical library.

Visited the Z.I.B. (Central Institute fur Bibliothek, Swesen) Central Institute of Librarianship and introduced to one of the chief staff members, Dr. Irmgard Dressler. This institute is under the Ministry of Culture and the Director of this institute advises the Ministry about their requirements for the development of public libraries in G.D.R. This institute runs a school of librarianship for training middle level library workers needed for public libraries. There are three levels of library courses in G.D.R. a) Apprenticeship, b) Librarians and c) Scientific research and academic librarians. According to public library system, the entire country is divided into 15 districts and each district is sub-divided into sub-districts and sub-districts into towns. This institute brings out good number of publications.

On 2nd March, 1981, I was taken to Karl Marx University Central Library and showed all the sections within the Library. This library has more than two million eight hundred thousand books and monographs ; theses and dissertations/700 thousand ; Printed music/29 thousand ; Autographs/and hand written letters 1,00,700 ; Portraits 11,500 ; Maps and Atlases 3,000 ; Periodical subscription 6,700. The Acquisition section of this library is headed by Mr. Klassig, one of the Deputy Directors. There are about 20 staff members working in this particular section and has exchange collaboration with 1,200 institutes and 37,000 books are added annually. A separate book Binding section (restoration section) is attached to it. The Karl Marx University Central Library has an independent user's section headed by Mrs. Conradi. The Main functions of this section are :

a) Local lending,
b) Inter lending,
c) Maintenance of reading rooms and stacks.

There are about 18,000 borrowers as per the register but the actual users are only 6,000. Stock verification is not done and according to them it is an impossibility because of huge stocks. Secondly because of closed access system they presume the losses would be negligible. The time consumed for stock verification is much more and the needed result would be only a negligible loss of books.

With regard to exchange of books the type of books (books, journals, or thesis) and value (irrespective of currency) are not the criteria. The circulation section has an up-to-date, modern, electronic charging system, by which the issue and return transactions are done at a greater speed.

The Social Sciences Division of the Karl Marx University Library is situated at a distance of 3 kilometres in Karl Marx Plaza. This is an ultra modern library building built in 1978 (a tallest building with 28 storeys in the city) equipped with all sophisticated electronic systems of charging. This branch library has a capacity of 500 thousand books in three floors of the stack area. There are about 18,000 users in this library.

On the 4th of March, I visited the University of Commerce Library, Karl Marx Plaza, and met the Director Dr. Beyer. He is good enough to take me round the library. Most of the books collected and housed are related to trade and commerce. This institute was established in 1969. Before 1969, this was one of the Departments of the Karl Marx University, but later it became an independent institution to serve the specialised personnel in the field of economics, trade, foreign relations and commerce. This library has about 55,000 books with an annual addition of 5,500 books. It subscribes 489 journals on special fields of commerce. There are about 2,000 students in this University.

Another branch of library of Karl Marx University Library is department of Biological Sciences which was visited, possesses 24,000 books 223 current journals and 500 users.

In this city of Leipzig, I was taken to another special library called Deutsch Zentral Bucherei fur Bliende (Central Library for the Blind people) established by the government of G.D.R. and supposed to be one of the best in Europe. In the whole of Europe it is the only institution, well-organised for the handicapped, particularly to the blind. There is also an organisation for the blind people namely the International Association for the Blind and this institution is a member of it. This library was established in the year 1894. This was moved to the present building in 1954. This is the only library in the Republic of G.D.R.... This library was also not spared in the World War—II. This was also damaged and a few books were either stolen or destroyed. This very first book published was on religion. There are about 7,000 titles and 27 thousand tomes in German language. This house published various types of suitable monographs (brailey system). Since it is also a publishing concern, there are many divisions namely Printing, Binding and Proof-Reading departments. All the departments are well organised with the latest and sophisticated equipments namely brailey typewriters, latest printing machinery, cutting, binding and backing machinery.

Most of the reading materials are recorded in tapes which are supplied for home reading in the form of cassette. Regarding brailey books there are two main types namely *Scattering*—the old type and the other is *Copying*—a new type. There is a fantastic and sophisticated studio attached to this institution. This studio is similar to any other T.V. studio with all the latest auditory systems to record programmes given by the blind for the benefit of the blind.In G.D.R., there are about 32,000 blind people out of which 2 per cent are children up to 16 years of age and 70 per cent are old people. There is also a special test to examine and assess whether the blindness occurred by birth or by accident. This is done by the association of blind people to enroll them as members. Apart from teaching programmes for the blind, there is also a postal correspondence course available cheaper. About 2000 customers visit in a year and avail the services of the library. This is a new institution under the Ministry of Culture.

On 9th March, I visited the Stadt Bezeriks Bibliothek (town public library). This library is under the Ministry of Culture. This is an independent regional public library. Mrs. Weisshaupt is the head of this library. As a regional library, it has around it 37 libraries of various types including children's libraries and 247 librarians are employed. The book stock is one million and current journals subscribed are 350 ; Phonograms and tapes one lakh ; pictures 4,600. About 1 lakh 6 thousand people make use of the library in a year and 3,00,000 books are being lent a year. In all the public libraries 'Kinder Section' is a speciality. Specially designed children's books are displayed and also issued. This children's section possess about 8,000 titles and 2,000 children visit a month, and 14,000 books are being lent per month.

Then I visited Teknik Hocschule Bibliothek (Library of the Technical High School). The Director is Mr. Faeschke, and the Interpreter Mrs. Kerner. This Library was established in the year 1977. Earlier to 1977, this institution was called as 'College of Civil Engineering.' Book stock is 1,20,000 ; standards 5,000 ; Poligraphy 1,500 and University dissertations and diploma papers 8000 ; Journals subscribed are 500 ; total staff is 50 ; number of students 1200 ; teachers 600. The annual additions are 6000 a year. Exchange of books with 469 partners and practicals with 29 partners. This is the institution affiliated to the technical University of Dresden (GDR).

Visited the Deutsch Bucherai of Leipzig (National Library of G.D.R). I was introduced to Dr. Pomsaal Gerhard, Vice-Director General of the Library who was also the past Vice-President of IFLA, and chaired a session of 'Bibliography.' According to him this was originally a Prussian Royal Library founded in 17th century (1661) and became an International Archives of G.D.R. in 1912. Here, I was introduced to Dr. Butrmann, Head of the Department of the Library school. I had a detailed discussion with him and his staff with regard to the courses, syllabus in Library Science. Next, I was taken round the library by Mr. Gittel Herbert one of the Deputy Directors of the library. I am very much impressed to see the stack area, reading hall, exhibition hall, Map section, Technical section, and Issue Counter. This is very old library established 400 years ago. This is a well constructed, well designed and fantastic in its appearance. A new extension of multiple stack area with all modern equipment is under construction. The stack area and the circulation section is connected with electronic book trolley and pnuematic information system. The bibliographic section headed by Mrs. Jesche has been doing a real service to its readers. They compile (1) Regional Bibliographies translated from Russian, (2) Bibliography of German books published in other countries with cumulative indexing (quarterly), (3) National Bibliography (weekly)—computerised. Another important section of the library is the Music collection. This section is headed by Mrs. Gebruser. This section is unique in the sense, since 1943 such of those musical records as are needed by research scholars, musicians and persons interested in music are being collected. An exhaustive Author and Subject Bibliography is compiled in two volumes. The total collection is 1,70,000. This is exclusively a reference library. Twelve members of staff are working in this particular section.

On the concluding day, I was introduced to Dr. Heinz Hohne, Head of the catalogue division and also to the Vice-President of IFLA. We had a detailed discussion on the preparation of catalogue and cataloguing usage in GDR libraries. He is responsible for the following publications: a) International development in the sphere of alphabetical cataloguing since the IFLA conference 1961. b) Rules for alphabetical cataloguing (RAK) in 4 volumes published by Bibliothek-Swesen, Berlin 1976.

Halle-Saale a small town is about 50 kilometres from the Leipzig city. There exists a University called 'Martin Luther University.' This was founded in 1694. The library was founded in 1696. Originally, this library was a gift and donation made by the land lords of Halle. This is originally called Lands—Bibliothek and latter became the University library. This University is specialised in medical sciences. All the medical students of G.D.R. prosecute their studies in this university after getting through the German language test. This central library has 2 million 300 thousand books and the other departmental libraries put together have about 1 million 300 thousand books. The field of specialization is cooperation with the department of Ecology and bring out certain bibliographies in those disciplines. The library compiles a regional bibliography of the area as well publishes the recent additions list. There are 17,000 users including teaching staff. In the University proper there are 8,600 students and 2,500 staff.

Library of German Oriental Society, Halle was established in 1846. In the Second World War, most of its oriental literature was either destroyed or stolen away. In 1945, this library was clubbed with University Library of Halle. This library has 55,000 volumes. Very rich and rare and valuable materials are housed in this section. Quite a good number of Dravidian language books are available. A good catalogue is also made available for consultation. Old paper manuscripts, a few palmyra leaf manuscripts, and writings on copper plates and other media are also available. A small museum of rare collection and materials are stored in in this house. Very old bibliographies of Asian Studies is also made available.

Dresden : This is one of the biggest industrial cities of G.D.R. Very well-planned Technical University is established in this city. This University has a Central Library with 26 divisional libraries. This was founded in 1826. Dr. H.D. Winstting, Deputy Director of Technical University Bibliothek Dresden took me round the Central Library, as well as one of the Divisional Libraries. This library has one million 200 thousand books ; two million patents ; 300 thousand standards and specifications ; 6000 titles of journals are subscribed and with an annual addition of 30,000 books. There are 12,000 direct students and 3,000 part-time students ; 4000 teachers are teaching. The Library staff members are 220. The charging system is with data processing. The booklets published by this University Library are History of Technical University Library ; Students' Hand Book ; Students' Library and Latest additions.

Sachsische Lands-Bibliothek, Dresden (*Public Library*) : This is an institution under Public Library System. This Library is an ancient library established in 1450 with special reference to Social Sciences. Prof. Dr. Burge-Meisher took me round the entire library and showed me various activities of it. This has a social cooperation with industry, trade users and workers. This library has more than 1 million 50 thousand books ; 4000 titles of periodicals on subscription and about 250 library staff.

In addition to books, there are about 16,000 Musical texts and 30,000 Records. The special collections are Saxonian Bibliographies in all the fields of Literature and Stenographic collection. A book exhibition in this library is unique in the sense, varieties of books belong to earlier centuries, incunabula, original manuscripts, specially bounded material are displayed under lock and key.

My visit to G.D.R. was concluded between 25th and 27th of March, in visiting the Institute of Library and Information Science of the Humboldt University and giving a few lectures to the students of the department. The director of this institute along with the staff had a detailed discussion with regard to curriculum and syllabus of their courses.

General Observation : I am highly thankful to the U.G.C. for nominating me to visit G.D.R. under the scheme of Indo-GDR Cultural Exchange Programme. I am equally thankful to G.D.R. government for receiving me affectionately at their end and showing me the libraries, museums and all schools of Library Science and other cultural centres. Apart from the people and places of G.D.R., the Cultural centres which I have visited are fantastic. I found very good coordination and cooperation between the academic and public libraries.. Even the Ministries, namely the Ministry of Culture (Public Library) and the Ministry of Higher Education (for academic and technical Universities) have also a very good understanding in chalking out the future plans from prosperity. There are three schools of library science to impart courses for three levels of librarians needed for their country. The German library association and the Director of libraries advises the Ministry of Culture with regard to the public library activities. The German State Library in Berlin and the National Library at Leipzig do serve the public at large at national level. The academic libraries mostly the University libraries are headed by the Directors (librarians) who are responsible for the Technology of Higher Education are advised by the Ministry of Higher Education.

Methodical centre for Scientific Library and Information and Documentation research is a special institution which evolves forms and standards with regard to staff, building, furniture and services required by academic as well as public libraries.

In general, I enjoyed my visit of three months in Berlin and other major cities with the utmost satisfaction in understanding the culture of the country.

Suggestions

1. There is an imperative need to have a network of public libraries for the entire country from village level to national level with regional libraries at most suitable regional centres.

2. In view of correspondence courses and allowing the employees to sit for the examinations privately from Inter to P.G. Courses, there is absolute necessity to have proper coordination between public libraries and academic libraries.
3. Areas of cooperation should be identified between academic and public libraries and action taken with due consent witn Ministries concerned.
4. There should be a national level organization to direct all the library systems (Public, Academic and Special libraries) in suggesting suitable norms and standards with regard to staff, building, equipment and technical work.
5. The major public libraries and the university libraries should introduce automation to speed up the services in the areas of cataloguing, bibliography, charging systems and information services. To start with a few University libraries may be introduced with a few mechanical devices as an experimental basis, choosing a few from the south and a few from the North.
6. The courses of the library schools should be restructured with need based study with due relevance to type of libraries where the students function rather than on more theoretical study.
7. The students of Library and Information Science should be made to work as apprentices in various types of libraries (depending on their choice between Public, Academic and Special Libraries) to have a thorough practical orientation before they embark into the profession.
8. A thorough research should be made at the national level on 'users' study in all the types of libraries and suggest the libraries to cope up with the required services.
9. *Need for a centre for library equipment* : For the benefit of the Librarians and Libraries, one library should be selected in a region and all the necessary library equipment essentially required and to be acquired by the libraries and should be preserved and displayed in one of the halls of the centre, to choose the most suitable and choicest piece of item required by the library. For this, the manufactures of library equipments in the region may be requested to donate one piece of each of the items to the regional

centre for proper display and exhibition and place orders with their choicest firm. This practice is in vogue in England.

10. There is need to equip the academic libraries particularly the University Libraries with the following minimum equipment towards extension activities to contain the students to make use of the libraries in their leisure hours for purposes of recreation, and cultural development :
    (a) Micro-filming equipment ;
    (b) Micro-film readers ;
    (c) Photocopying equipment ;
    (d) Audio-visual equipment like Film projector and T.V., Tape recorder with cassettes ; record player with ear-phones ; Gramophone discs, recorded speeches of eminent scientists, social-scientists and literary luminaries ; recorded speeches of Convocation addresses delivered by eminent persons in different Universities.
    (e) Culture representing dance, drama and music, both classical and modern in the form of books and recorded cassettes to be collected.

ROUND THE LIBRARIES
United States

At the outest let me thank the university authorities for giving me permission to attend International Conference of ALISE at Chicago between 15-17 January, 1985 and thereafter to visit different States in U.S.A.—its various types of Libraries, schools of Library Science and Museums up to 15th February, 1986.

Enroute to Chicago, I have to make a halt for five days from 9th to 14th at New York and in Pennsylvania State College (Philadelphia). On 9th, 10th and 11th I could utilise my time satisfactorily in visiting United Nations Library and U.N.O. building, New York Public Library and New York University Library. I have made a detailed study in different sections of those libraries and what impressed me very much was the oriental section of the New York Public Library which was computerised on line search programme in Asian languages , and secondly, the computerised circulation system in the University Library.

In Pennsylvania State University Park/State College Library, I was introduced to the Dean of University Libraries who was good enough to spend two hours with me in exchanging views. As head of Libraries, he was good enough to take me round his libraries and showed the Acquisition Section, the Cataloguing Division, Periodical Wing and Circulation Area which are operated through computers. The search for a catalogue of books and other documents is not through the conventional catalogue (up to 1979) but the search is made through T.V. Monitors with the help of key boards connected to the main computer data base. The other interested area in this university is the "LIAS" (Library Information Access System)—

an innovation to search library information net works are integrated to Library system made by Dr. Gordon Nebb Rawline, Assistant Dean of Libraries.

On 14th Afternoon, I arrived at Chicago and lodged at hotel Palmer where the venue was arranged for "ALISE" Conference. I have not only attended the conference but very much involved in the group discussions from 15th to 17th January, 1986. The theme of the conference is "Accredetation the way ahead". There are about 300 delegates from various parts of the globe. There was one representation each from India, China, Japan, West Germany for the conference. There were many interesting groups to discuss on the following topics (viz.) :

> Stress management ; Continuing Education ; Student Activity ; Teaching Methods ; Retirees ; Curriculum/Library History ; International Library Education ; Research ; On line Education and Women in Librarianship.

The entire proceedings were lively, heartening, thought provoking and highly interesting to discuss various problems at utmost care without any fear or favour.

From 18th to 20th ; in addition, I was also invited by Mr. Roger H. Perent, Acting Executive Director of A.L.A. to attend their mid-winter meeting as their guest and to have opportunities to confer with many Library Colleagues attending this meeting. About 2000 delegates from all over the U.S.A. have participated. The entire conference was divided into 20 different groups for administrative reasons. I had participated in one particular group namely "Role of Archives in the University Library set up", presided over by Francis O. Mattson, Curator of rare books division of the New York Public Library, New York.

On 19th January 1986, I visited Chicago University Library, Public Library and Museum and observed the functioning of the above Libraries and Museums which are excellently managed for the use of the visitors.

On 20th January, 1986, I left to Visconsin (Madison), on 21st, 22nd and 23rd instants, I visited Madison Memorial Library, Department of Asian Studies and Department of Library & Information Science.

On 24th and 25th, I visited Springfield (Illinois) Lincoln Memorial Library & Museum. The Lincoln Home is one of the most significant historic sites associated with America's beloved sixteenth President. It is the only home Ahraham Lincoln ever owned. Lincoln Home National Historic site encompasses four city blocks in down town Springfield, Illinois surrounding the Lincoln Home.

Also visited the Sangamon State University Library, Springfield, Illinois wherein the whole library collection is housed in four levels viz. 1. First (Lower) level : Archives/Special collection, University records, Illinois regional Achives, depository, Media Lab and Services Wing (Copier, bending machines, Typewriters etc.) 2. At the second (Main) level : Collections, catalogues, Indexes and Abstracts, Microficho Collections, slides, references collection. services like Book returns cards catalogue, copying machine, 'get help here' desk, Microform readers and printers, study areas, online searching, photo duplication service etc. 3. At the third level : Collection of games. Newspapers and periodicals, services like Art gallery, current periodicals, Browing Area, Microform readers, study areas etc. are placed here.

At the fourth level collections viz. General book collection, kits, oversize book collection and services like lockers, study areas, telephone to 'get help here' desk also provided here. In this building itself, Department of Library Training, class room is located.

26th—27th January : Visited UCLA Biomedical Library, University of California, Los Angeles which primarily serves the school of Medicine and Biomedicines. Also, it is open for use by the general public. All Library users have free access to the open stock collection. The outstanding feature of the collection is the strength of its periodicals holdings both current and restrospective. The Library also has an excellent reference collection, a comprehensive historical section and gives special emphasis to the fields of neuroscience, psychiatry, ophthalmology, radiation biology, molecular biology and vertebrate zoology. Increased emphasis is being given to the acquisition of audio-visual materials. The UCLA Library Information system—ORION is a computer file containing records of most books acquired and catalogued by the UCLA Library System since 1977. ORION on line can be consulted via public terminals in the card catalogue area of the Reference Reading Room.

28th—29th January, 1986: Visited Library of Congress (National Library of USA) Washington DC ; which has its services spread over world wide. Congress accepted in January 1895 Former President Thomas Jafferson's offer, appropriating $ 23,950 for collection of 6,487 books. Thus the foundation was laid for a great National Library.

The Library of Congress Complex on Capitol Hill includes three buildings. The Thomas Jefferson Building, executed in Italian Renaissance style, is the oldest of these. In 1897, decorated with splendid sculpture, murals and mosaics created by 50 American Artists. The main reading room, which can be viewed from the visitor's gallery, soars 160 feet from floor to dome. The room houses a collection of 45,000 reference books, a portion of the extensive main catalogue of more than 23 million cards and desks for 212 readers. The adjacent computer catalogue centre provides public access to the Library's automated catalogue files through computer terminals.

Secondly, the simply designed, dignified John Adams Building, faced with white Georgia marble, was opened in 1939. Bas relief sculptures on its large bronze doors represents 12 historic figures credited with giving the art of writing to their people.

Thirdly, the White Marble James Medison Memorial buildings, dedicated on April 24, 1980, more than doubled the Library's available Capitol Hill space. Here, eight reading rooms, exhibition areas, offices, and storage area for the library's special format collections, which number over 50 millions items.

Collections of the Library of Congress include almost 50 million items convening virtually every subject informats that vary from papyrus to microform. These materials stretch along 532 miles of shelves and are being acquired at a rate of ten items a minute. The library has 20 million books and pamphlets in some 60 languages and more than 35 million manuscripts relating to treasures of American history and culture as the papers of Presidents, notable families, writers, artists and scientists. The Library has the world's largest and most comprehensive cartographic collection—almost 4 million maps and atlases, dating back to the middle of the 14th century—and a 6 million pieces music collection that includes autograph scores, correspondence of composers and musicians, flutes from throughout the world. Approximately 75,000 serial titles are received annually : 1,200 newspapers are held in library's permanent collection. There are also half a million sound records, more than 250,000 reels of motion pictures, and over three millon microforms.

The Library of Congress provides numerous services which directly or indirectly benefit all Americans. A primary role is to serve as the research and reference arm of the Congress. Through the Congressional Research Service (CRS), a department established over 60 years ago, the library provides legislators with the information they need to govern wisely and effectively. The staff of CRS answers more than 300,000 inquiries a year. In addition CRS prepares bill digests, summaries of major legislations and other reference tools to help members and their committees stay abreast of the daily flow of legislation.

The copyright office in the Library of Congress administers the operation of United States Copyright law, a major force for the encouragement of library and artistic endeavours.

Library of Congress provides scholarly resources as its most important service to the scholarly community, scholars, public, writers, teachers, artists, journalists, students—any one pursuing serious research—may use the library's reading rooms, each of which has a catalogue of reference collection, and reference librarians to guide the way. Readers may use computer terminals to search the library's data bases for new titles, sources of information of subjects and for legislative histories.

I also visited Smithsonian Institution, an independent federal agency, holds in trust for the nation some 100 million artifacts and specimens. The institution, an important centre for research, is dedicated to public education, national service and scholarship in the arts, science and history. It was established in 1846 with funds bequeathed to the United States by James Smithson an English scientist. When we visit any of the Smithsonian's, 13 museums or the National Zoo, we are entering the world's largest museum complex. The Institution also include these entities, separately administered by their own boards of trustees: The National Gallery of Art, the Woodrow Wilson International Centre for scholars and the John F. Kennedy Centre for the Performing Arts.

The National Air and Space Museum, mostly visited in the world, gives people a sense of participation in the evaluation of air and space technology. Featured are special films on a five-story-, high movie screen and insights into the workings of our universe during presentations in the space arium.

The Samuel P. Lengley Theatre presents "The Dream is Alive" offers an insider's view of America's space programme. We can see astronauts at work both inside and outside the spacecraft : the development of scientific and communications satellites, the dramatic capture and repair of the "Solar Man" Satellite and the first space walk by an American Woman astronaut, Kathy Sulivan.

On 30 January, 1986—1st Feb., 86, I visited Boston University

Library, Boston Public Library and Harvard Medical and Law Libraries.

The Frances A Countway Library of Medicine opened in 1965 and houses the combined collections of the Harvard Medical Library (est. 1782) and the Boston Medical Library (est. 1875). Holdings exceed 500,000 volumes, including 4,500 active journals. The journals (non-circulating serials) holding lists are available at reference desks microfiche in reference area and for location majority shelved alphabetically in first floor and some titles are listed in catalogue and shelved by call number and on 2nd floor. The Abstracts and indexes (subject/author guides to journals articles) holdings listed by subject/Title in card catalogue. The psychological Abstracts, Dissertation Abstracts, Chemical Abstracts, Biological, Abstracts current contents, index medicus are on the subscription of the library. Regarding the holdings of books they are listed by subject/author/title in the card catalogue. Government documents holdings and location will be listed by publication number/agency/title in card catalogue are on 2nd floor, some HEZO publications are on microfiche in reference area ; those listed by publication number or series in serial records office are on 3rd floor.

Apart from usual services i.e. regulating access to the library and issuing of borrowers cards, charging out books (loan period 2 weeks), renewing of book loans to walk-in people or by phone, determining whether a book is charged out or missing, briefly holds requested material for individuals, the library also stores course reserve books and examination review books. The Library holds audio-visual and head sets for use in A/V carrol room. Rare books, special collections pertaining to the history of medicine. In the reference division, the library offers computer searches and copy service for staff-mediated photocopying adhering to copyright law—240/exposure and also provides self service photocopying machine—104/exposure.

On 2-2-86, from Boston I returned to New York, and reached Bombay on 3rd, from there on 4th instant reached Madras by fligt. From Madras I reached Tirupati by Train. On 6th Feb., 1986, I reported to duty and resumed my routine duties as Librarian & Head of the Department of Library & Information Science, S.V. University, Tirupati as usual.

In this connection, finally, I thank each and everybody of those who have helped me and encouraged me for my successful trip to Chicago for attending ALISE Conference and for active participation in the conference deliberations and group discussions at International level. Really, it is thrilling experience for me to visit the libraries in the States and observing latest trends and techniques in the field of library and information science that they have already adopted. The Techno services, computer usage in retrieval of information organisation of various types of libraries and the methods they follow suits conditions, depicting the social, cultural and educational activities of those people in the respective places.

It will be only a dream for Indians since we are living in a developing country. The financial resources will not permit us to upkeep the modern libraries of India on the lines of US libraries. To conclude, I can express my personal view that we the Indians are not lacking with the abreast of latest knowledge and methods in the field, but we are lacking in financial resources and latest equipments since we cannot afford to have them at this stage. The remaining services, organisation in libraries, teaching methods in library science of India are superb when compared to US libraries. The time consciousness (personality), sincerity among the people and dedicated effective service that they provide to the readers can be appreciated at length.

INDEX